PRESS FOR ACTION

Religious Education: FESTIVALS

Lynne Broadbent
Jan Thompson

Folens
Publishers

Contents

© 1994 Folens Limited, on behalf of the authors.

ISBN 1 85276308-6

Illustrations by Eric Jones.
Cover by Abacus Art.

First published 1994 by Folens Limited, Dunstable and Dublin.
Folens Limited, Albert House, Apex Business Centre, Boscombe Road, Dunstable, LU5 4RL, England.
Printed in Singapore by Craft Print.

Introduction

The study of a festival offers pupils a valuable opportunity to develop their knowledge and understanding of a religion's history, key beliefs and present rituals.

Festivals are a common source for RE teaching in primary schools, where pupils hear and act the 'festival story', make greetings cards and taste festival foods. It is not that these activities are inappropriate for older children - indeed, they are part of a community's celebration. However, RE at secondary level should offer something more. This book contains a wide variety of activities at different levels which seek to develop a depth of knowledge and understanding. They focus upon:

- understanding the importance of AUTHORITY in religion, through key figures and holy books

- understanding SYMBOLISM in religion through ritual

- understanding WORSHIP and CELEBRATION both in the home and within the wider faith community

- exploring ULTIMATE QUESTIONS (e.g. sin and forgiveness with Yom Kippur, victory over death with Easter)

- exploring VALUES and LIFESTYLES (e.g. in the Jewish home at Shabbat)

- the celebration of a festival within a faith community: the period of preparation; the idea of celebrating in the present by remembering the past and looking with hope towards the future; the involvement of the individual and the whole community and the role of women.

These activities are not designed to be the sole resource for teaching about a festival. They are intended to supplement input from the teacher, from video, artefact, poster and textbook, and provide a means of helping pupils focus upon key issues which lie at the heart of each festival.

Festivals sheet

Some features of festivals are common to all religions:
- there is usually a time when the family or the believers prepare before the festival begins
- usually special stories are told at the festival
- the family, or believers, remember a special person or event.

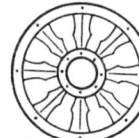

Other features are different:
- the festival may be celebrated for one day, or more
- the festival may be celebrated at home, in the place of worship, or in both places
- special clothes may be worn
- special food may be eaten, or songs sung.

 Record some information about festivals. Note similarities and differences. Find the information from books, posters, videos and from interviewing people from different faiths.

FESTIVAL	RELIGION	STORY/ STORIES	SPECIAL EVENT/ PERSON	WHERE CELEBRATED	FOOD, CLOTHES, SONGS, etc.
e.g. Shabbat	Judaism	Creation	Friday meal	Home and synagogue	two loaves of bread, wine ...

continue over the page...

Teachers' notes

BUDDHIST FESTIVALS

Page 6. WESAK

Wesak, the main Buddhist festival, celebrates the birth, enlightenment and death of the Buddha. Pupils could be introduced to the founder of Buddhism and his fundamental teaching through the festival of Wesak. It is also a festival of light. Studying this festival could reinforce and deepen understanding of this important religious symbol.

A symbol, mentioned on page 6, is the lotus flower. This beautiful bloom is often seen gracing stagnant ponds - something beautiful growing out of the mud below. In Indian religions the lotus symbol teaches that purity, goodness and spiritual enlightenment can come out of the earthiness of human life. For Buddhists, the Buddha is the prime example of someone who is believed to have reached the peaks of spiritual existence in this earthly life. Flowers, cut flowers especially, represent to Buddhists the impermanence and changing nature of life. Living things, like flowers, grow, decay and die. Buddhism teaches that it is important to come to terms with the fact that we too shall die.

The Buddha began life as a prince, but four signs dramatically changed his life. The signs are easy for pupils to remember because they all start with the letter 'D'. The prince saw a sick man (Disease), an old man (Decay), a funeral procession (Death) and a holy man (who practised self-Discipline). These broadened his experience of what life was about and disturbed him so much that he set out on a quest to make sense of it all. He started from the premise that all life involves suffering, and found a way of coping with it. This is summarised in the Four Noble Truths, which are fundamental to Buddhism (see page 7). Ask pupils to think of examples where suffering disappears, when people no longer crave for things to be different but simply accept what life brings. Are there also examples where this is **not** true? Do they agree with the initial premise that 'All life is suffering' - not just in terms of physical pain and deprivation, but also in the sense of not finding complete fulfilment in what we do?

Followers of the Buddha believe that he became enlightened and reached the state of Nirvana. That is why he is called 'The Buddha' which means 'The Enlightened One'. Because of this, light is an important feature of Wesak. Light is a universal symbol of hope and goodness. Pupils could explore the idea of 'seeing the light' as in the Buddha's enlightenment.

Page 7. THE BUDDHA

The Noble Eightfold Path is central to the Buddhist way of life. It aims to decrease and ultimately to stop all desire and therefore suffering.

Right View is the acceptance of the Four Noble Truths.

Right Intention is the commitment to give up the way of desire and follow the Noble Eightfold Path.

Right Speech means that Buddhists should be careful how they use their words, avoiding lying and slander, and only speaking with kindness and respect. Pupils could make lists of good and bad uses of speech.

Right Action involves keeping the Buddhist Five Precepts: not to kill, steal, be unchaste, lie or take drugs of any kind. You might discuss further with your pupils what each of these rules involves.

Right Livelihood means that Buddhists should not break any of the five precepts in the way they earn their living. Ask pupils to think of jobs which would be forbidden to Buddhists, e.g. working as a butcher (this is involved with taking life).

Right Effort and the last two steps are concerned with a Buddhist's spiritual life and control of the mind, which is achieved through regular meditation. Buddhists must make a conscious effort to think good thoughts at all times.

Right Mindfulness is being fully aware of thoughts and feelings so that you can be in control of them.

Right Contemplation leads to complete peace and fulfilment, called Nirvana - the goal of Buddhism.

Wesak

The festival of Wesak is the most important Buddhist festival, celebrating the birth, enlightenment and death of the Buddha.

● Complete the picture story of Gautama Buddha's life and talk about the importance of the events to Buddhists.

Activity

Gautama's mother dreamed a white elephant touched her side with a lotus flower and her child was conceived.	Prince Siddhartha Gautama was born into a noble Indian family. He led a rich and sheltered life.

At 29 the Prince saw a holy man who had renounced the world to find truth. In the real world, Gautama saw sickness, pain and death. He gave up his lifestyle to find out why.	At 35, as he sat in meditation under the Bodhi tree, Gautama was enlightened. He found the answer which made sense of life to him - the Four Noble truths.

● Why is Wesak a festival of light?
● Why is the Buddha often shown seated on a lotus?

The Buddha

Gautama saw how much suffering there was in the world. He knew that even he, who had everything, would have to die. He became more troubled. Finally he left home to try to find peace of mind by following the way of the Indian holy men. He gave up everything and, for six years, lived a life of extreme self-denial. But he was still not content.

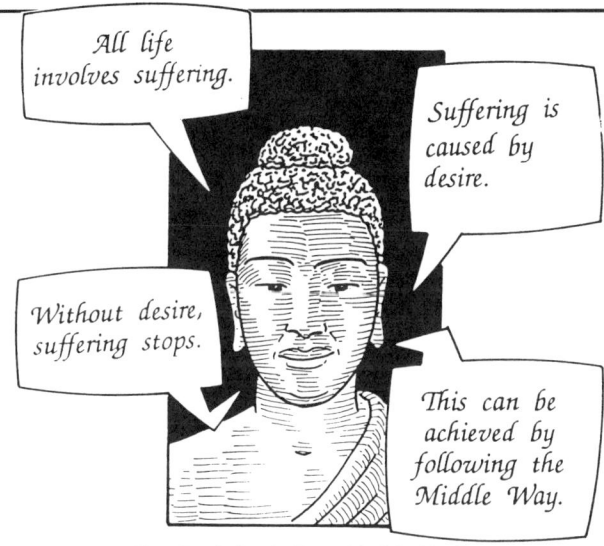

All life involves suffering.

Suffering is caused by desire.

Without desire, suffering stops.

This can be achieved by following the Middle Way.

The Buddha's Four Noble Truths

So he rejected this way also, ate a good meal and sat down under a tree in meditation. There, he discovered his answer to life - the **Four Noble Truths**. He knew that life involved suffering, but he came eventually to understand that suffering is caused by our wanting it to be different. If we stop wanting, then we stop suffering.

He set out the **Middle Way** in eight steps, known as the **Noble Eightfold Path**: Right view, Right intention, Right speech, Right action, Right livelihood, Right effort, Right mindfulness, Right contemplation.

Activity

- Work in pairs. Discuss the Noble Eightfold Path. Write on the signposts what you think each would mean to a Buddhist.

Teachers' notes

CHRISTIAN FESTIVALS

Page 9. CHURCH CALENDAR

The answers are: Pentecost - Easter - Advent - Christmas - Lent - Epiphany - Ascension.

Page 10. CALENDAR COLOURS

The answers are: Advent and Lent. About a quarter of the year is spent in celebration (Christmas, Epiphany, Easter, Ascension and Whit Sunday).

Page 11. CHRISTMAS PREPARATION

There will be a variety of answers here, e.g. Jesus is the Christian Saviour, Lord, Son of God ... Christianity teaches that Jesus Christ is divine - part of the Holy Trinity of God.

An Advent wreath made with plastic holly leaves should last for many years in your RE artefact collection.

Page 12. CHRISTMAS - JESUS

Jesus is at the centre of Christmas. Begin by discussing how this Christian emphasis is often obscured by the secular nature of much of Christmas celebration.

The **second circle:** (a) Joseph (b) King Herod and the Wise Men (c) the angel and the shepherds (d) Simeon (e) Anna.

The **third circle:** (a) see Mark 3: 16-19 for a list of the twelve disciples (b) see Luke 8: 3 for some of Jesus' women followers (c) many Bibles have lists of healing miracles at the back; or see Mark 1: 21-2: 12 for a number of examples (d) Jesus taught the disciples, the crowds, e.g. the 5 000, and individuals, e.g. Nicodemus in John 3 (e) Jewish groups included the Pharisees and Sadducees.

The **outer circle:** examples of Church denominations are Greek Orthodox, Roman Catholic, Church of England, Methodist; examples of famous Christians are Mother Teresa, Sybil Phoenix, Cliff Richard, Cicely Saunders, Desmond Tutu, Jackie Pullinger.

Page 13. CHRISTMAS CELEBRATION

The bread and wine of Holy Communion stand for the body and blood of Jesus Christ. The nativity account in Luke's Gospel tells of the shepherds, and Matthew's account includes the wise men.

Page 14. EASTER PREPARATION

The order is: Shrove Tuesday, Ash Wednesday, Lent, Holy Week, Palm Sunday, Maundy Thursday, Good Friday, Holy Saturday.

The Lenten fast is based on Jesus' fast in the wilderness. Palm Sunday recalls Jesus' triumphal entry into Jerusalem when the crowd went out to meet him, waving palm branches. The foot washing of Maundy Thursday re-enacts Jesus' washing of the disciples' feet. 'Good' Friday is so called because Christians believe it was necessary for salvation.

Page 15. EASTER CELEBRATION

The Paschal candle stands for Jesus the Light of the World (the bringer of hope and spiritual enlightenment). Christians light their own small candles from the Paschal candle to show that he is the source of their 'light', and they pass the light from one to another to show their readiness to share the Good News of Christianity with each other.

Page 16. SUNDAY

Encourage pupils to think about the question of Sunday opening from the point of view of the people who are employed to serve in shops on Sunday. What effect may this have on family and religious life? Look at the needs of people who patronise shops which are open on Sundays.

Page 17. PENTECOST

The dove symbolises peace, purity and gentleness. The symbols for the Holy Spirit in the account of the first Whitsun are wind and fire. The 'fruits of the spirit' are love, joy, peace, patience, kindness, goodness, faithfulness, gentleness and self-control. Take the idea of the fruit-bowl and make a large picture for display.

Church calendar

This Church calendar is used by Anglicans and Roman Catholics. In addition to the festivals and seasons shown on the diagram, they also celebrate Sundays and Saints' Days. The Eastern Orthodox Churches also observe the Church's year, but some of these churches follow a calendar which is thirteen days behind the common Western one (so their Christmas falls not on 25th December but on 7th January). Other Churches may only celebrate Sundays and the three main Christian festivals of Christmas, Easter and Pentecost.

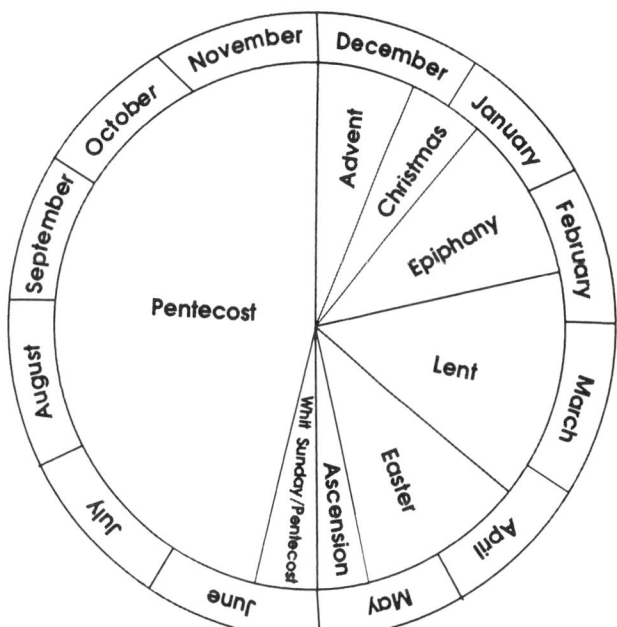

Activity

- Using the Church calendar, write the name of the season or festival against its correct description below.

The birthday of the Church, when the power of the Holy Spirit was given to the disciples (also called Whitsun).	
The celebration of the death and resurrection of Jesus Christ.	
The time of preparation for the 'coming' of Christ.	
The celebration of the birth of Jesus Christ.	
The period of preparation for Easter. Forty days to remember Jesus' forty days without food in the wilderness.	
The 'showing forth' of Jesus to the world beyond the Jews (represented by wise men from the east).	
The 'going up' of Jesus into heaven to reign with God in glory.	

Research

Which Christian festivals fall on the same day each year. Which dates vary? Why do some change?

Festivals on same day each year + date	Festivals whose dates vary

Calendar colours

The Church uses colours to express the moods of different festivals and seasons in its calendar.

It uses:
green for growth in the Christian faith.
violet for solemn times of preparation before important festivals.
white or **gold** for big celebrations.
red for Pentecost or Whit Sunday (to represent the fire of the Holy Spirit) and for Saints' Days (for the blood of the martyrs).

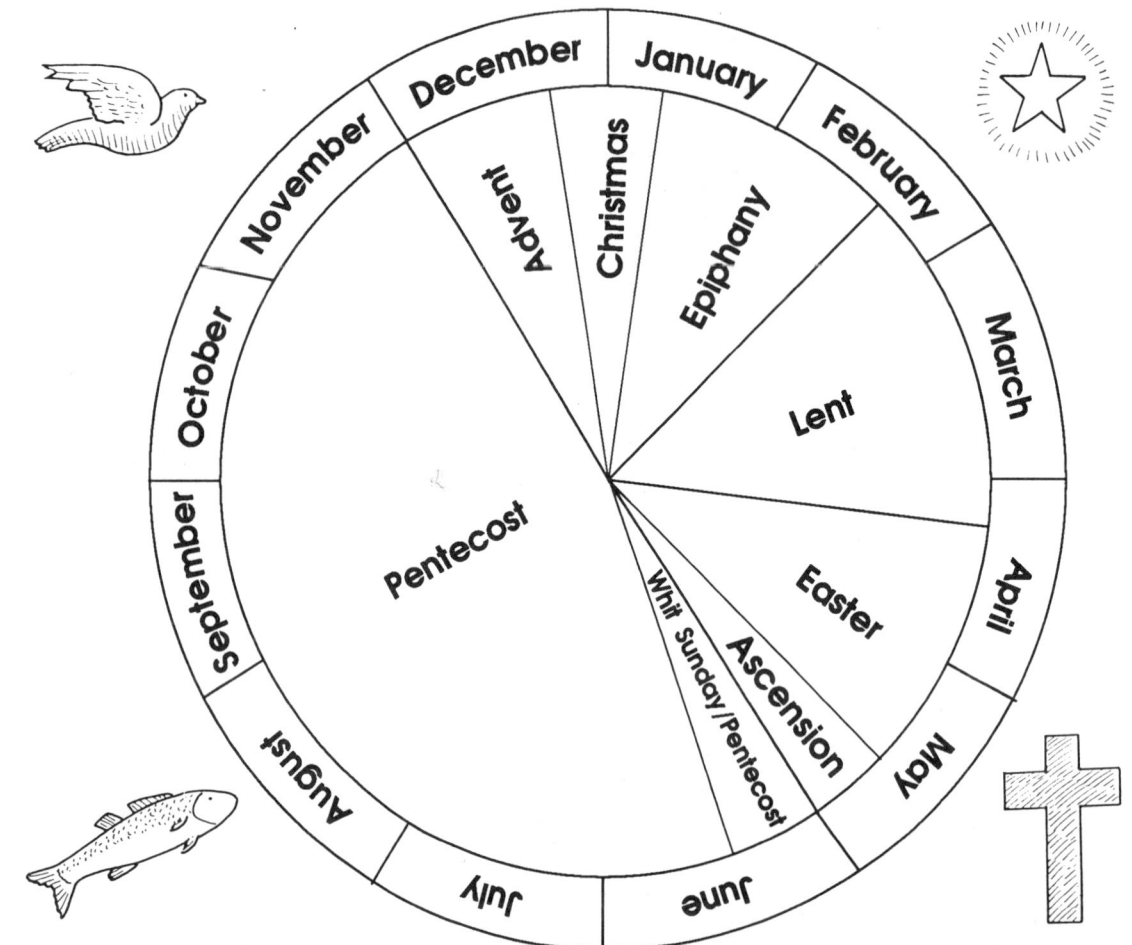

Activities

- Colour the diagram using:
  - **violet** for Advent and Lent
  - **white/gold** for Christmas, Epiphany, Easter and Ascension
  - **red** for Pentecost/Whit Sunday (**not** the big period of Pentecost!)
  - **green** for the main period called Pentecost.
- Discuss the moods that these colours suggest to you.

- Find Christmas and Easter on the diagram. Notice the long periods of preparation for Christians before these two important festivals. What are these periods of preparation called?
- Calculate how much of the Church's year is spent in celebration rather than preparation for festivals.

Christmas preparation

Christmas celebrates the birth of Jesus Christ 'The Light of the World,' on 25th December (in the Western Church). Advent lasts for about a month beforehand. Christians make a special effort in their religious lives to prepare themselves for this great event.

Many Christians believe that they should prepare themselves during the Advent season so that they can really appreciate the meaning of the birth of Jesus Christ.

They might make an extra effort to pray, to go to church, and to discuss their faith with others. They might run fund-raising events for charity and make a special effort to do good.

An Advent wreath is a circle of evergreen leaves with four small candles in it (preferably purple - the church's colour for Advent) and a large white candle in the middle. The small candles are lit on each of the four Sundays before Christmas, and the large candle is lit on Christmas Day (so that, by then, all five candles are alight).

Activities

- Advent is an old word meaning arrival or coming. What are people waiting for?
- Make an Advent wreath, using a ring of Plasticine decorated with plastic evergreen (holly, etc.) and four small candles. Press this on to a firm cardboard base and fix the candle in the middle with some more Plasticine.
- Discuss what you think the individual items which make up an advent wreath symbolise:
  - four small candles
  - large central candle
  - lights
  - evergreen leaves
  - a circle.

  Fill in the table opposite. Compare your answers.

- Do you and your family make preparations for Christmas? If so, make a list of them and illustrate it if you wish. In what ways are these preparations 'religious'?

AN ADVENT WREATH

Item	Symbol
four small candles	
large central candle	
lights	
evergreen leaves	
a circle	

- Read the story of the birth of Jesus in the Bible:
  Luke 1 : 26-35   Luke 2 : 1-20
  Matthew 2 : 1-12.
- Why is Christmas so important for Christians? What do they believe about Jesus' birth? Who do they believe he is?

NOW

Christmas - Jesus

This diagram starts at the centre with the birth of Jesus to Mary. It then works outwards, showing how Jesus influenced more and more people in the world.

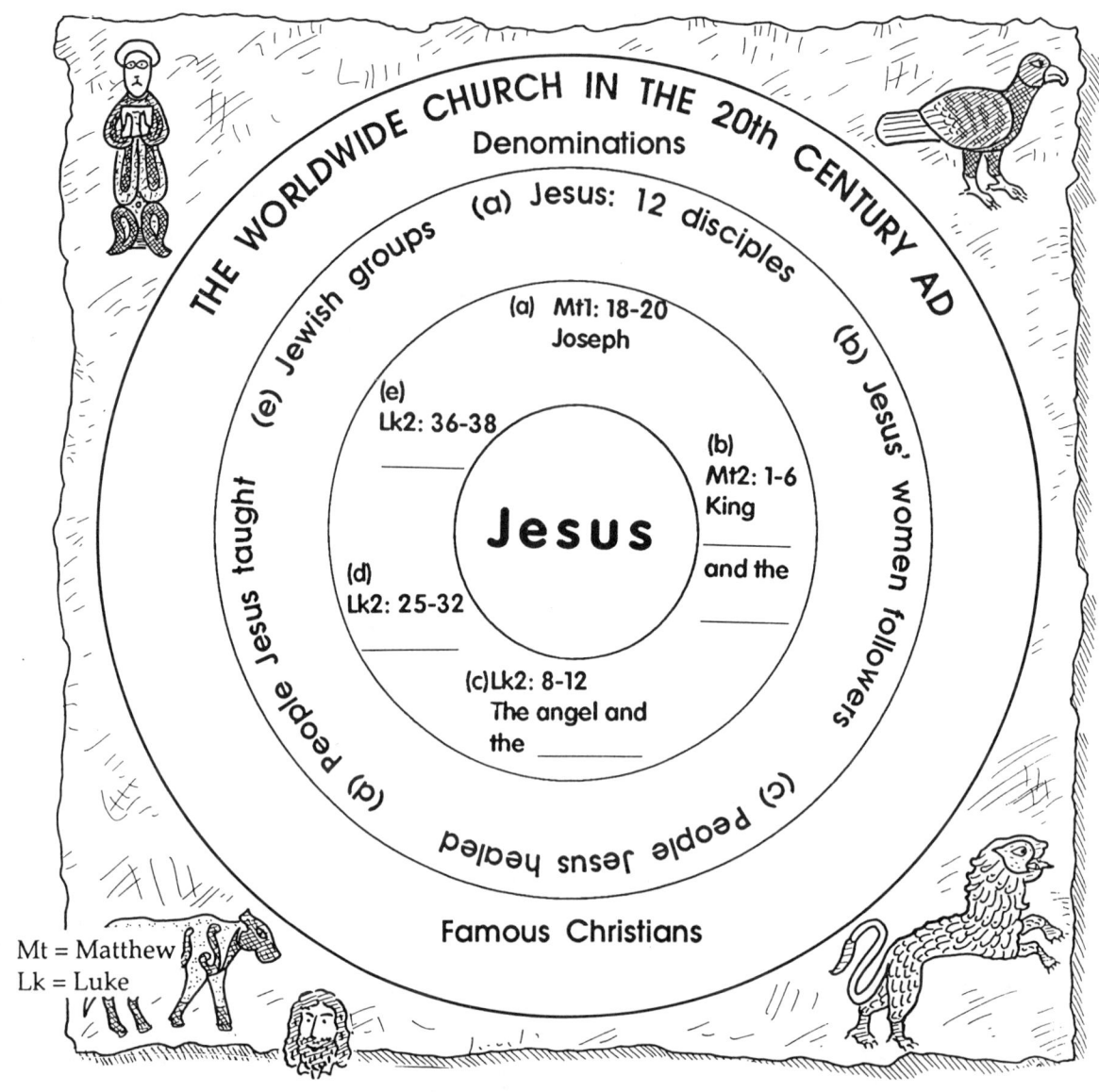

THE WORLDWIDE CHURCH IN THE 20th CENTURY AD
Denominations

(a) Jesus: 12 disciples

(e) Jewish groups

(b) Jesus' women followers

(c) people Jesus healed

(d) people Jesus taught

Famous Christians

(a) Mt1: 18-20 Joseph

(e) Lk2: 36-38 _____

(b) Mt2: 1-6 King _____ and the _____

(d) Lk2: 25-32 _____

(c) Lk2: 8-12 The angel and the _____

Jesus

Mt = Matthew
Lk = Luke

Activities

- Look up the Bible references in circle 1. Write the names of the people affected by the baby Jesus. The first example is done for you.
- In circle 2, name some examples in each group (a - d).

Research

- The outer circle represents the world wide church today. Name some church denominations and some well known Christians of the twentieth century.

Christmas celebration

Focus To consider some of the ways that Christians celebrate Christmas.

MIDNIGHT MASS
Many Christians are gathered in church at midnight, so that their first act on Christmas Day is to receive Holy Communion. This helps them to feel closer to Jesus.
● What do the bread and wine of Holy Communion stand for?

BIBLE READINGS
Matthew 1-2
Luke 1-2

● Read chapter 2 from both Matthew's and Luke's Gospels. Which contains the story of
(a) the shepherds, and which has
(b) the Wise Men?

CAROLS
● Research the history of carols and then write out a verse from a Christmas carol which speaks about the birth of Jesus.

CANDLES
In the Bible, Jesus is said to be the 'Light of the World'.
● What do you think this means?
● Where can you see special candles and other lights at Christmas?

CHARITY
Jesus was not born in the palace where the Wise Men expected to find him, but in a stable. This was a sign that he was to devote his life to the poor. Christians, following his example, often give to charity at Christmas. Special collections may be taken at Christmas services. Sometimes people bring presents to put under a Christmas tree in church, to be distributed to a children's or old people's home. Sometimes people go out in the streets to collect money by carol singing.
● Research a named charity and explain what it hopes to achieve.

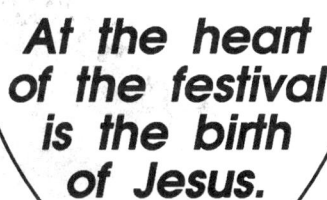

At the heart of the festival is the birth of Jesus.

GIFTS
Christians believe that Jesus is God's gift to the world.
● Who brought gifts to worship the baby Jesus (Matthew 2: 7-12)?
● Are you hoping for something special this Christmas?

Easter preparation

To **see** how events in the Bible have influenced Christian practices today.

Forty days of Lent →

| Shrove Tuesday | Ash Wednesday | Holy Week | Easter Sunday |

Activities

- Work in groups. Cut out the eight boxes and arrange them in the correct order of events. Read the Bible passages as indicated to answer the questions.

LENT is the time of preparation for Easter.
- Ask five Christians if they keep Lent, and if so how (some may be doing extra things rather than giving up anything). Share your answers.

ASH WEDNESDAY. This is the first day of Lent. It is called Ash Wednesday because of the practice of daubing ash on people's foreheads as a sign of penitence.
- Read the words spoken by the priest as he puts ash on your forehead. Choose one word each to express how this makes you feel.
  'Remember that you are dust and to dust you shall return.'

PALM SUNDAY. Holy Week starts with Palm Sunday.
- Read John 12 verses 12-19 and say why this day became 'Palm' Sunday. How do churches celebrate it? Jesus entered Jerusalem humbly on a donkey. How might you expect a king to enter his capital city?

GOOD FRIDAY. This is the day when Jesus was crucified. It is the saddest, most solemn day of the year for Christians. Some churches hold services from noon to 3pm - the time of Jesus' death.
- Read this Church of England prayer. Notice particularly how it ends, and say why you think this sad day is called 'Good' Friday.
  Almighty Father, look with mercy on this your family for which our Lord Jesus Christ was content to be betrayed and given up into the hands of wicked men and to suffer death upon the cross; who is alive and glorified with you and the Holy Spirit, one God, now and for ever.
  Amen.

SHROVE TUESDAY is Pancake Day. Traditionally pancakes were made to use up the fat before the fast of Lent. What event in Jesus' life does this practice of fasting recall?
- Read Matthew 4 verses 1-2.

HOLY WEEK. This is the week leading up to Easter Day. During this week church services help Christians to relive the final events of Jesus' life, and so feel closer to him in his suffering.

MAUNDY THURSDAY. In Britain, the Queen gives out Maundy Money to a pre-selected group of people. It used to be the custom for the monarch to wash the feet of some poor people.
- Read John 13 verses 1-5 and explain why foot-washing is connected with Maundy Thursday.
In the evening of Maundy Thursday a Holy Communion service is held to recall Jesus' actions at the Last Supper when he left his followers something to remember him by.
- What two things did Jesus leave them? Read Mark 14 verses 17 and 22-25.
Many churches stay open for a further hour of quiet prayer when the service is over, or sometimes for several hours until midnight. This recalls Jesus' time of prayer in the Garden of Gethsemane when he asked his disciples to stay awake with him. Did they?
- See Mark 14 verses 32-42.

HOLY SATURDAY. This day recalls the time that Jesus' corpse lay in the tomb. Evening services on this day look forward to the following day - Easter Sunday - the day of Resurrection.
- Read Mark 16.

PFA Religious Education: FESTIVALS. F3086 © Folens.

Easter celebration

Focus To show how hope can grow out of despair and how symbols express this for Christians.

The sadness of Good Friday gives way to the joy of Easter Sunday as Christians celebrate the Resurrection of Jesus Christ from death and his return to God.

Activity

- Read the verses from Matthew 28 verses 1-10 and underline the words from the hymn below (**A**) which echo this passage.

The Sabbath was over, and it was about daybreak on Sunday, when Mary of Magdala and the other Mary came to look at the grave. Suddenly there was a violent earthquake; an angel of the Lord descended from heaven; he came to the stone and rolled it away, and sat himself down on it. His face shone like lightning; his garments were as white as snow. At the sight of him the guards shook with fear and lay like the dead.
The angel then addressed the women: "You," he said, "have nothing to fear. I know you are looking for Jesus who was crucified. He is not here; he has been raised again, as he said he would be. Come and see the place where he was laid, and then go quickly and tell his disciples: He has been raised from the dead and is going on before you into Galilee. They will see me there."
They hurried away from the tomb in awe and great joy, and ran to tell the disciples. Suddenly Jesus was there in their path. He gave them his greeting, and they came up and clasped his feet, falling prostrate before him. Then Jesus said to them, "Do not be afraid. Go and take word to my brothers that they are to leave for Galilee. They will see me there."

Matthew 28: 1-10

A

Lo, Jesus meets us, risen from the tomb,
Lovingly he greets us, scatters fear and gloom;
Let the Church with gladness, hymns of triumph sing,
For her Lord now liveth, death has lost its sting.

(100 Hymns for Today, No. 95)

NOW

- How does the last line of this hymn show the relevance of Jesus' resurrection for Christians today?
- Some Christians say that Jesus lives in their hearts. What could they mean by this?
- A crucifix has the figure of Jesus on the cross. How does a plain cross represent both Jesus' death and resurrection?
- In Roman Catholic and some Anglican Churches a large Paschal (Easter) candle is brought into the dark church on Easter Eve and everyone there lights their small candle from it. What do you think this represents?
- What do Easter eggs represent?

Sunday

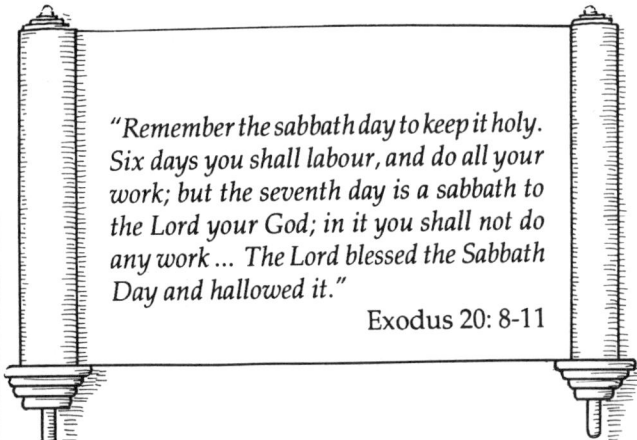

"Remember the sabbath day to keep it holy. Six days you shall labour, and do all your work; but the seventh day is a sabbath to the Lord your God; in it you shall not do any work ... The Lord blessed the Sabbath Day and hallowed it."

Exodus 20: 8-11

There is no doubt that this commandment to keep the Sabbath Day has influenced the Christian holy day. But the Jewish Sabbath is on the seventh day of the week, whereas the Christian holy day is Sunday, the first day of the week.

The most important thing about the Christian Sunday is that it is 'The Lord's Day' (Revelation 1: 10) - a celebration of the Resurrection of the Lord Jesus Christ. The name *'Sunday'* refers to Jesus as the 'Sun of Righteousness' (Malachi 4: 2), the 'Light of the World' (John 8: 12).

Activities

- List ways you think Sunday is different from the rest of the week.
- There has been considerable debate recently over shops which have broken the Sunday trading laws by opening on a Sunday. Consider the arguments for and against Sunday opening, thinking about it from different people's point of views.

FOR	AGAINST

Research

As a class, work out questions for a survey of how Christians spend Sundays. Try to find out what religious value this day has for them. Ask questions of three Christians each, and share your findings with the rest of the class. List any important results from the class research.

Extra Idea On the notepad are three reasons for having a special day set aside each week. Discuss them with a partner and then put them in order of importance by numbering them 1-3 with number 1 as most important.

Time for prayer and to worship God.
A day of rest, to unwind and relax.
Time to spend with the family.

Pentecost

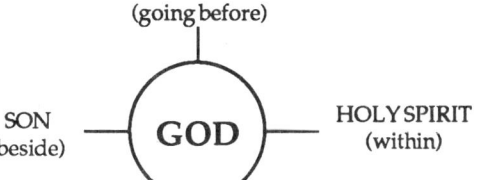

FATHER
(going before)

SON
(beside)   **GOD**   HOLY SPIRIT
(within)

A very important teaching in Christianity is that God is One and yet known to us in three ways. God is said to be a Trinity, i.e. three in one.

Many people can picture God the Father (the Creator) and God the Son (Jesus Christ) but find it difficult to imagine what God the Holy Spirit is like.

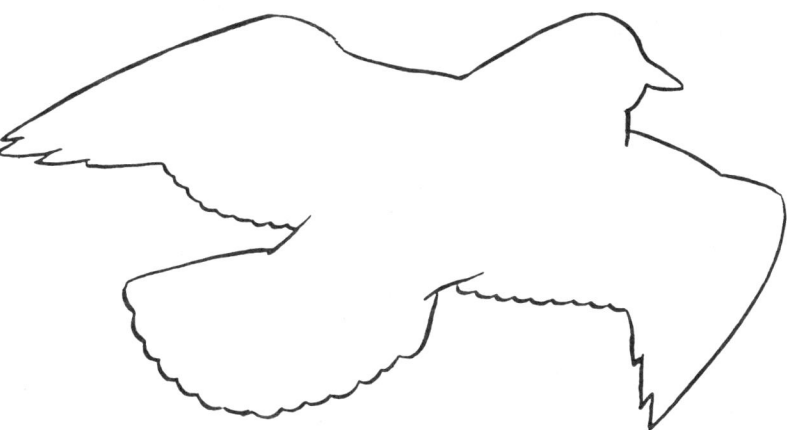

Activities

Acts 2: 1-4 Symbols for The Holy Spirit.

_____

_____

- A dove is a popular symbol for the Holy Spirit. What ideas does it suggest to you? Write them inside the shape.
- Read Acts 2 verses 1-4. Name the two powerful symbols for the Holy Spirit found in this passage.

Extra Ideas

- The Quakers are Christians who teach that there is a spark of God the Creator in everyone. What do you think of this idea?
- Name the nine 'fruits of the Spirit' from Galatians 5 verses 22-23 in the fruit shapes. Talk about what they mean.

Although Pentecost (or Whitsun) is the third most important of Christian festivals, unlike Christmas and Easter, it usually passes unnoticed outside the Church. Yet it is the birthday of the Church, when the Holy Spirit is said to have inspired the early disciples to carry on Jesus' work on earth.

Today, Christians still speak of the Holy Spirit working among them and within each of them. They claim that the Spirit gives them their faith, helps them to know what God wants them to do with their lives, and gives them strength to cope with all that life brings.

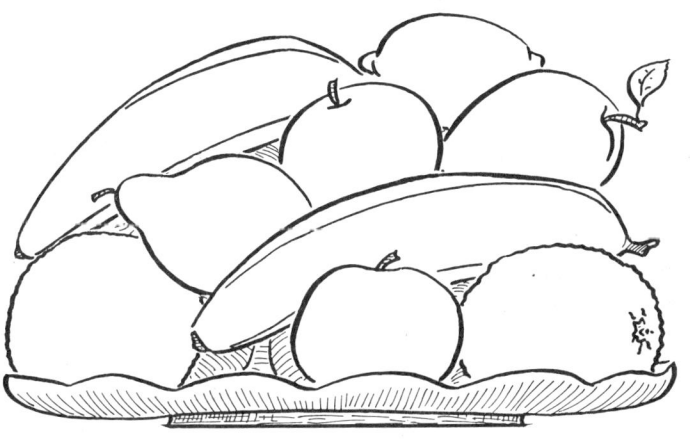

Teachers' notes

HINDU FESTIVALS

'Hinduism' is a Western title to cover the diverse ancient religious traditions of the vast sub-continent of India. Within this there are three main foci of devotion:
- Vaishnavism - the worship of Vishnu
- Shaivism - the worship of Shiva
- Shaktism - the worship of Shakti, the Mother Goddess.

There is also talk of a trinity of gods (although their descriptions are an over-simplification):
- Brahma - the Creator
- Vishnu - the Preserver
- Shiva - the Destroyer.

What Westerners find difficult to understand, and what is important to teach pupils, is that essentially Hindus believe in ONE GOD ('Brahma'). Their many deities (and many things in the created world) speak to them about different aspects of God's nature. But for most Hindus, it is not so much the beliefs that matter as the religious practices which intermingle with their daily lives. It is therefore a usual approach to study the religious practices in Hindu festivals.

There are countless festivals in India: local, regional, North/South and a few national ones. These are celebrated in different places in different ways. So do not be surprised if you discover alternatives in the books you use in class or the experiences of your pupils. The three major festivals which tend to be celebrated throughout India (though in diverse ways) - Divali, Holi and Navaratri - have been chosen. The first two of these are Vaishnavite, so that pupils will come to understand something of the nature of God represented by the kindly god Vishnu. Navaratri is worship of the Mother Goddess and a particularly important time for women, emphasising that festivals are for all sections of the community, women and children as well as men and religious leaders.

Page 19. DIVALI

Since many pupils will have discussed Divali in Primary school, only one sheet on this has been included and the focus is on its connection with the Goddess Lakshmi rather than the over-familiar story of Rama and Sita. There are many common features of festivals here, e.g. getting oneself washed and dressed; cleaning and decorating the house, e.g. with paper chains; exchanging cards and presents; feasting, music and dancing; fireworks; wishing people wealth and prosperity for the new year. Some pupils may also mention customs like leaving the door ajar at New Year for the 'first footer' or the Jewish custom of leaving the door ajar for Elijah at Passover. There are many aspects of Divali celebrations that pupils could make for a class display: divas; Indian food, sweets; paper flower garlands or paper-chains; greetings cards; rangoli patterns (begin in the centre and work outwards symmetrically - there is often a lotus/water-lily motif in the centre).

Page 20. NAVARATRI

This tackles the difficult area of Hindu deities and tries to discourage ideas of Hinduism as a polytheistic religion. It also raises the distinction between images and idols. It is amazing that so much trouble can be taken over making the image of the Mother Goddess, and so much care lavished upon it in worship, and yet when it is finished with, it is immersed in a river or pond. Durga's power is indicated by her riding a tiger, by having eight arms, and by all the weapons she holds.

Islam and Judaism do not attempt to depict God, both for fear of idolatry and because God must be greater than anything we can imagine. Yet they do have word images for God. Islam has the ninety-nine Beautiful Names of God from the Qur'an, e.g. 'The Judge', 'The Light'. The Jewish Scriptures speak of God as 'King of Kings', 'Rock of Salvation', etc. See especially the Book of Psalms.

Page 21. HOLI (pronounced as 'holy')

This emphasises the excitement of the bonfire celebrations and the good-natured merriment that goes on with the coloured water. Many Christians have a very stern image of God which leads both to guilt that they are not living up to his standards and to fear of punishment. The playful Krishna helps Hindus to see another side of God's nature which may encourage pupils to broaden their ideas of the way people think about God. Questions ask pupils to describe God in words rather than draw a picture of God since this would not be permissible to many Muslims or Jews.

Divali

Divali means 'row of lights'. It is a Hindu winter festival. In northern India it recalls the famous story of Rama and Sita: in southern India it is a time to worship Lakshmi. Rama and Lakshmi are connected with the kindly god Vishnu. Lakshmi, goddess of wealth and good fortune, is his wife, while Rama is said to have been an appearance of Vishnu on earth to destroy an evil demon.

Activity

- Read the text around Lakshmi. Fill in the missing words in the passages.
  Choose from: light; songs; prosperity; feasting; welcome; clothes; windows.

People prepare themselves to receive Lakshmi by bathing and dressing up in new _____ .

The celebrations include music and dancing. _____ of welcome are sung for the goddess.

Buildings are lit inside and out with rows of clay lamps (divas) and strings of electric lights. Celebrations involve sparklers and firework displays. This is to welcome the goddess and to _____ her way.

The goddess is worshipped with prayers and the offering of food. This is then shared out so that everyone can share in her blessings. It is a time of _____ with family and friends. Special Indian sweets are very popular at Divali.

Homes are cleaned and then decorated with garlands of flowers or paper-chains. At the entrance, rangoli patterns are made from red, white and yellow powders or chalks. This is done to _____ the goddess. _____ are left open for the goddess to enter.

Divali marks the end of the financial year, when businessmen settle their debts and close their accounts. They ask Lakshmi to bring them _____ in the coming year. Divali greetings cards wish people good fortune. Presents are also exchanged.

- Underline any of the above customs in which you have taken part at non-Hindu celebrations.
- Find out about either rangoli patterns or making a Divali card.

Navaratri

Hindus believe that there is one God; but to help them understand the many different aspects of God's nature, they speak of gods and goddesses. They believe that God who created both men and women has both male and female characteristics. Navaratri is a special festival in praise of the Mother Goddess, who is represented in different ways, e.g. as Parvati she is gentle and kind, but as Durga she is powerful and fearsome. Durga is shown holding weapons given to her by different gods to slay a demon.

A special image of the Mother Goddess is made for this festival, which is used in worship. On the final day, this image is taken in procession to the river (sacred to Hindus) and immersed in the water. The festival is over and the image has served its purpose. The image itself is not God - but it has reminded the worshippers of God's motherly nature during this festival for the Mother Goddess.

Activities

- Write down the first six words that come to mind when you think of the word 'mother' or 'motherly'. Share them with your group. Are they all words describing mothers as kind and welcoming?
- As well as a gentle side, mothers need to be physically strong. Why?
- Look at the picture of Durga and **colour** all the things which show her as powerful. Explain why.

- Make a list of objects, images or symbols in other religions which help people to understand what God is like.

Religion	Object	Meaning
Christianity	Crucifix	God loved his people so much he suffered for them.

- Can you name any religions or denominations which forbid images of God? Why do you think they do this?

Holi

Holi is a Spring festival. It often lasts two days and is a New Year festival, seeing out the old year and welcoming in the new.

The name Holi comes from Holika, the demon aunt of Prince Prahlad. She tried to kill the boy in a blazing fire, but she herself was burnt to death instead. A bonfire is a central part of Holi celebrations. Sometimes an effigy of Holika is burned on the fire, to show that evil can be destroyed. When it is alight people process around it and roast coconuts and popcorn to eat as 'prasad' (holy food because it has been offered to God).

In India, the next day is a day of fun, when red powder is thrown and coloured water is squirted over friends and any passers by. This day of good-natured mischief reminds Hindus of the pranks of Krishna when he was young. Krishna is said to be an appearance of the god Vishnu, who comes to Earth to help in times of need and to restore goodness and justice.

(A)

Activities

- What English festival also involves the burning of an effigy? What does this celebrate?
- If you have ever celebrated around a bonfire, write words in the flames of **A** to express how it made you feel.
- Can you think of any other occasions when people share holy food together?
- Holi suggests the interesting idea that God is **not** all solemn. If you think of God as a person do you ever imagine God to be smiling or laughing? Describe the image of God that you have in mind.

Religion	Holy food
Hindu - Holi festival	Prasad

The story of Holika

Focus   To reinforce the story behind the festival of Holi.

This is a story of good overcoming evil, and of God's loving care for his faithful worshippers.

A demon king was jealous of his son's devotion to the god Vishnu and did everything in his power to stop it. When Prince Prahlad refused to give up his religion, his father even tried to kill him, but to no avail. When a wild elephant was set loose on him, the young boy bravely approached, chanting the name of Vishnu, and the elephant meekly knelt in submission before him. Even being thrown down a steep ravine, and into a flooded river, did not succeed in killing the boy. It merely increased his faith. Finally, Holika, the king's demon sister, grabbed the boy and jumped with him into a fire, believing that she would be magically protected. As the flames died away, it was discovered that Holika had perished but the boy Prahlad was unharmed.

Activity

- In India, Hindus are fond of comic-strips like the one below. Read the story and then fill in the speech bubbles using your own words.

Teachers' notes

ISLAMIC FESTIVALS

There are not so many festivals in Islam as in other religions. Three important ones are discussed here. Others which are also celebrated by all Muslims commemorate important events in the life of Muhammad (pbuh, peace be unto him), e.g. New Year's Day - the Day of the Hijrah - since this was so important in the history of Islam.

Page 24. RAMADAN

Ramadan is the time of preparation before Eid-ul-Fitr without which this festival of fast-breaking makes no sense. The questions encourage pupils to think about the significance and implications of fasting, ie days are longer in summer and it is difficult to go without a drink; on the other hand, people often do not want to eat on a hot day, but need food more in the cold of winter.

The final questions ask pupils to think about themselves. They suggest situations which would give exemption from fasting in Islam, e.g. if age is a factor. Muslim children will gradually accustom themselves to fasting. At about the age of ten, they may fast for a full day once or twice during the month. They will not be expected to do the full fast until they are adults, i.e. have reached puberty. In Islam, you would not be expected to fast if you were ill. Islam makes exemptions for people on journeys, or soldiers in war.

Page 25. EID-UL-FITR

This sheet lists various aspects of Eid-ul-Fitr which pupils should recognise from other contexts. The first example is Christian, but pupils may also give secular examples common to celebration, e.g. they could mention birthday presents.

Instructions are given for making an Eid card. The two Arabic examples, with the clever calligraphy, are taken from inside Muslim cards.

Page 26. EID-UL-ADHA

The emphasis here is on sacrifice, both its meaning today and the more traditional example of animal sacrifice. The story at the heart of this festival is that of Ibrahim (Abraham) and Ishmael (Isaac).

It is important to show the links between religions, such as the common heritage here between Islam, Judaism, and Christianity (and interesting to see the differences). Pupils may also have easier access to a Bible than to an English interpretation of the Qur'an, in order to read the story for themselves.

There is often debate in the media over the ritual slaughter of animals both in Islam and Judaism, and pupils may be able to collect some articles to help with this discussion. Although the slitting of any animal's throat sounds barbaric, these religions claim that their methods are more humane than those allowed in modern abattoirs. Questions encourage pupils to think about the morality of killing animals for meat, and to consider ways in which animals are treated, both in their rearing and killing.

Page 27. NEW YEAR

Anno Domini is Latin for 'in the year of our Lord', so 1992 means 1992 years after Jesus' birth.

Ask pupils to think about the value of putting things behind them and starting again. Since some questions are quite personal, you need to be sensitive to the way that pupils are grouped (if at all) to answer them.

Ramadan

To appreciate the importance of fasting for Muslims.

Ramadan is a very special month for Muslims. It is when they remember God's gift of the Qur'an, their holy book. At this time they make a special effort to be good Muslims - thinking of God and being kind to one another. It is made different from all other months because it is **the month of fasting**. Muslims go without food and drink during the daylight hours of the whole of this month. They eat at night and very early in the morning.

Activity

- Consider carefully whether it would be more difficult to fast in summer or winter, and explain your answer.

Muslims keep to the fast of Ramadan because they are commanded to do so in the Qur'an, and because their Prophet Muhammad (peace be upon him) used to do it.

Keeping the fast helps Muslims:

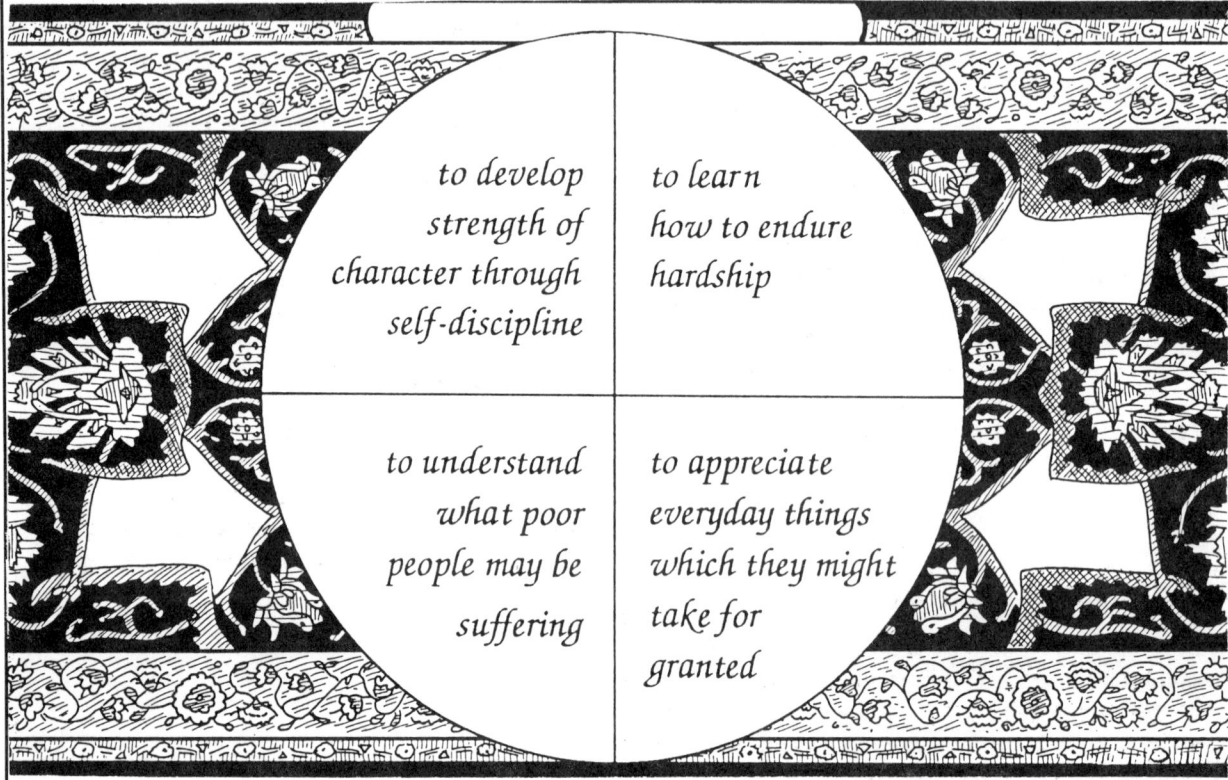

to develop strength of character through self-discipline

to learn how to endure hardship

to understand what poor people may be suffering

to appreciate everyday things which they might take for granted

- Look at the diagram and discuss with your group which of these four benefits of fasting is most important. Write numbers 1-4 in the arrows, with the most important being number 1.

NOW

•• Discuss •• **Think about yourselves.**

- Do you think you are old enough to take part in such a fast?
- Are there times when it would not be healthy for you to go without food and drink for a long time?

Not all Muslims are obliged to fast. For instance, it would not be healthy for a pregnant woman to do so. Some Muslims will not be able to keep the entire fast but may be able to do a little of it.

Eid-ul-Fitr

Focus To see that the way Muslims celebrate Eid-ul-Fitr has much in common with the way people celebrate festivals generally.

Ramadan ends, and the next month starts when the new moon is seen after twenty-nine or thirty days. This is a time of great rejoicing. Muslims thank God for sending them their holy book, the Qur'an, for guidance, and for giving them the strength to complete the fast of Ramadan. Eid-ul-Fitr means Festival of Fast-breaking.

Activity

- Listed below are some of the ways in which Muslims celebrate Eid-ul-Fitr.
  Fill in the chart with similar examples of celebration of your own (not necessarily religious). The first example is given, to help you.

MUSLIMS	OTHERS
They attend a special morning service at the mosque.	Christians attend carol services at Christmas.
They give money for the poor to enjoy the festivities too.	
They give each other presents; children often receive money.	
They bathe and put on their new or best clothes.	
They meet with their families and friends.	
They have lots of their favourite foods.	
They send each other greetings cards.	

Extra Idea Make a card for Eid-ul-Fitr. It should open from left to right (because Arabic is written in the opposite direction to English). Decorate it in the traditional Muslim way, with geometric patterns. Use the greeting 'Eid Mubarak' ('Happy Eid'). Add a wish of your own.

أعاده الله علیکم وعلی المسلمین
جمیعًا بالیمن والکرامة والقبول

Wishing You the Blessings of Eid

أعاده الله علیکم ولعلی المسلمین بالعزة والنصر
BEST WISHES FOR THE HAPPY "EID"

Eid-ul-Adha

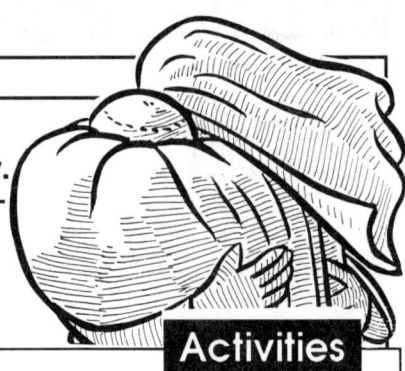

Focus To understand the meaning of sacrifice, and to compare versions of the same story.

At Eid-ul-Adha Muslims recall the ancient story of the prophets Ibrahim and his son Ishmael (peace be upon them). This father who loved his son so dearly was prepared to give him up for God.

Ibrahim was convinced by a dream that God wanted him to make a sacrifice of his only son. When he told Ishmael, his son bravely agreed that God must be obeyed. After they had prayed to God, Ibrahim laid his son face-downwards ready to kill him. But God called out and stopped him. There was no need for him to take his son's life for he had shown his readiness to fulfil God's commands.

To commemorate this story, Muslims make an animal sacrifice at Eid-ul-Adha. This costs a considerable amount of money, and the meat is shared out between family, friends and the poor.

Activities

- Discuss:
  - What is 'a sacrifice'?
  - Why do people make sacrifices?
  - What sacrifices might sports champions, parents and school children have to make?
  - Do you think their sacrifices are worth it?
  - Are they similar sacrifices as the one celebrated at Eid-ul-Adha? Why?
- Give other examples of people who make sacrifices. Write them below.

_____

_____

_____

After reading the Islamic and Jewish/Christian versions of this story about Ibrahim and Abraham, list any similarities and differences you can find.

MUSLIM VERSION	JEWISH/CHRISTIAN VERSION
(Qur'an Chapter 37 verse 100f)	(Genesis Chapter 22 verses 1-19)

" Discuss " ■ Whether you think it is right for people to criticise animal sacrifice if they are prepared to eat meat.

New Year

To understand the importance of dates and new beginnings.

New Year's Day for Muslims is the first day of the month of Muharram. On this day they recall the journey of their Prophet Muhammad (peace be upon him) from Makkah to Madinah in Arabia, where he set up the first Muslim state. This important journey is called the Hijrah, i.e. the 'migration' of the Muslims to Madinah.

Muslim years are dated from this event and are called AH for Anno Hegirae (in the year of the Hijrah).

CE stands for Common Era. It is a new way of referring to the common Western date which is now used by other people as well as Christians. So AD 1992 can also be written 1992 CE.

Muslims celebrate the New Year by attending a special service at the mosque, where they are reminded of the life of Muhammad (peace be upon him) and of his early followers.

New Year (1st Muharram) is a special holiday, but it is a religious day. New Year is a chance to turn your back on all that is bad in the past and to make some good resolutions for the future.

SAUDI ARABIA

Activities

- Look in an atlas. Label the map with the names of the countries, with Makkah, Madinah, and the route of the Hijrah.
- What does AD stand for, and therefore what does AD 1992 mean?
- Why should some religious groups prefer to use CE rather than AD?
- How does the Muslim New Year differ from some traditional western New Year celebrations?
- Think about these questions on your own and discuss them with a partner:
  - Try to remember any New Year resolutions you have made. Did you keep them? For how long?
  - What hopes do you have for the next year of your life?
  - What new beginnings have you had in your life, e.g. starting a new school?
  - Why is it useful to have new starts?
- Write some New Year Resolutions for next year.

New Year Resolutions

_____

_____

_____

_____

_____

_____

_____

_____

_____

Teachers' notes

JEWISH FESTIVALS

Within Judaism, the observance of most festivals is prescribed in the Torah. It is therefore a religious obligation to observe the festivals, it is not purely a matter of choice.

Jewish festivals begin the night before the day of the festival for in Genesis 'it was evening and it was morning...': night precedes the day. Therefore a festival runs from sunset to sunset. This allows an opportunity to explore with pupils the idea of sacred time, usually welcomed with the lighting of candles.

A festival may be celebrated primarily in the home (Passover), primarily in the synagogue (Yom Kippur) or in both places as is the case with Shabbat. Thus, within Judaism, the rituals observed in the home can be equally important to those marked in the place of worship, for both are fulfilling biblical commandments. This is of significance when considering the role of women. Festivals are often occasions for Jews in the Diaspora to focus upon the country of Israel. At Passover, the hope for future freedom for all Jews is encapsulated in the toast 'Next year in Jerusalem', while support for the Jewish National Fund and particularly its tree planting work in Israel is a feature of Tu Bi-Shevat.

Page 29. SHABBAT SHALOM!

The weekly festival of Shabbat is an important symbol of Jewish obedience to God and of Jewish identity. Pupils should understand that keeping Shabbat is a religious obligation. In some translations, the Exodus passage begins with 'Remember'. Thus the two candles represent the two commandments to 'Observe' and 'Remember' Shabbat. Shabbat, commencing at sunset, will begin at different times during the year. This raises the issue of needing to leave school and work early during winter months.

Page 30. SHABBAT WORSHIP

The Shema is written on a scroll, placed in a mezuzah and attached to the doorpost of a Jewish home. The rituals relating to the worship of God are for both the family and for the wider community. There is also free time to enjoy the company of others.

Page 32. THE PASSOVER SEDER

Missing are: Elijah's cup, two candles, a dish of salt water, an egg. **Blue:** Matzot (unleavened bread), often called 'bread of our affliction', is a reminder of the escape from Egypt. The Hebrews also ate lamb cooked with bitter herbs, so either the shankbone or the bitter herbs would be acceptable. **Green:** salt water and bitter herbs. See Exodus 12 verse 8 and also verse 15 for details of the future celebration of Passover. Unleavened bread is eaten because there was no time for the yeast to rise before leaving Egypt. The themes of Passover are oppression and freedom, both in the historical context and in the world today.

Page 33. ROSH HASHANAH and YOM KIPPUR

The story of Abraham and Isaac is one of obedience to God. In the Days of Awe between Rosh Hashanah and Yom Kippur, Jews repent for past wrongs and resolve to live in obedience to God.

Page 34. SHAVUOT

The Ten Commandments were a Covenant, or agreement, between God and his people, the Hebrews. When considering the influence of these today, it is important to recognise that the Ten Commandments underpin many values (laws) accepted within society and are observed by many people, including those of different faith traditions.

Page 36. SUKKOT

Sukkot is a harvest festival which also commemorates the journey of the Hebrews through the wilderness. The building of temporary shelters (sukkot) is a reminder of the temporary homes of the Hebrews and their dependence upon God.

Page 38. SIMCHAT TORAH

There is never an end to the reading of the Torah, so as the last passage of Deuteronomy is read in the synagogue, it is immediately followed by the opening of Genesis.

Page 39 and 40. HANUKAH

Mattathias' speech should stress a belief in God's presence in the struggle for freedom to worship. Lighting the hanukiah and displaying it in a public place is a symbol of freedom to worship. It also acknowledges God's help in attaining that freedom. The candles must be left to burn and their light cannot be used for work. The dreidel game originates from a much later period. When study of the Torah was forbidden, children if in danger of being discovered would immediately start playing dreidel. Thus it is fun but has serious origins. The Hebrew letters stand for 'Nes gadol haya sham' - 'A great miracle happened there' - and refer to a tradition which says that a small portion of oil lasted for eight days.

Page 43. TU BI-SHEVAT

There are many themes contained within this minor festival: awareness of the environment, links with Israel, actively working in the present for the future, and individual and collective hopes for the future.

Shabbat Shalom!

Focus

To understand Jewish belief about Shabbat and to recognise the symbols and practices which mark the beginning and end of this festival.

"Observe the sabbath day, to keep it holy, as I, the Lord your God, have commanded you ... Remember that you were slaves in Egypt, and that I, the Lord your God, rescued you."

Deuteronomy 5: 12-15

"Observe the Sabbath and keep it holy ... in six days I, the Lord, made the earth, the sky, the sea, and everything in them, but on the seventh day I rested. That is why I, the Lord, blessed the Sabbath and made it holy."

Exodus 20: 8-11

Read the following information about how Jews celebrate Shabbat.

On Friday evening Shabbat is welcomed like a bride into the home.
Just before sunset, the woman of the house lights two candles and says a blessing:
"Blessed are You, O Lord our God, Ruler of the universe, Who has made us holy by Your commandments, and has commanded us to light the Sabbath candles."
Everyone wishes each other "Shabbat Shalom".

At least two candles for two commandments are lit. Shabbat has begun!

Before the family meal a kiddush cup is filled with wine and raised by the father, who says this blessing:
"Blessed are You, O Lord our God, Ruler of the universe, Who creates the fruit of the vine."
This blessing 'sanctifies' or makes this day 'holy', separating it from all other days.

On the table are two loaves called challot, covered with a white cloth. A blessing is said:
"Blessed are You, O Lord our God, Ruler of the universe, Who brought forth bread from the earth."
Everyone eats some of the bread.

Activities

- Why do Jews celebrate Shabbat?
- Do some research and work out the approximate times for the start of Shabbat throughout the year.

Winter _____   Summer _____

Spring _____   Autumn _____

- 'Shabbat Shalom!' What does it mean? Why do you think this special greeting is used?
- The symbols of Shabbat relate to our senses. Match the senses with their symbol and meaning in the table.

	SYMBOL	MEANING
sight	lighted candle	
sound		
smell		
taste		

Shabbat worship

Read the Fact File about Shabbat.

FACT FILE

Jews worship in a synagogue.
There is a service on Friday evening.
The Shema is recited by everyone. It is from
Deuteronomy 6: 4-9 and contains the most
important Jewish beliefs.
There is also a service on Saturday morning
when the Torah scrolls are taken out of the
Ark. A different portion is read each week
and the whole Torah read each year. The
Torah is handwritten in Hebrew. In
Orthodox synagogues, the service is in
Hebrew; in Progressive synagogues, it is in
Hebrew and English.
Shabbat is different from other days of the
week. It is a time to leave weekly work
behind, a time of peace and joy spent with
family and friends and a time to worship
God together.
As the sun sets on Saturday evening, a short
ceremony is held in the home. Blessings are
said over a cup of wine, over spices in a
spice box and over a plaited candle, a
havdalah candle. As the havdalah candle is
put out in the overflowing wine, Shabbat
ends ... But the sweet-smelling spices are a
reminder of the sweetness of Shabbat.

Activities

- Find the Shema in Deuteronomy
  6: 4-9.
- Write it on the 'Torah scroll' opposite.
- Draw a six-picture diary of Shabbat events
  based on the Fact File.
- If you were to create your own special day of joy,
  peace and sharing with family and friends:
  - How would you spend it?
  - How would you begin and end your day?
  - What foods would you eat?

From slavery to freedom

Passover, or 'Pesach' in Hebrew, is a Spring festival. It celebrates a time when the Jews, then called Hebrews, were slaves in Egypt. Moses, directed by God, led the people out of slavery and persecution to the land of Canaan where they became free women and men; free to worship and to live according to God's laws.

Activity

- Paste the story on to the map in the correct order. Use a Bible to help you.
- Finish the story in your own words.

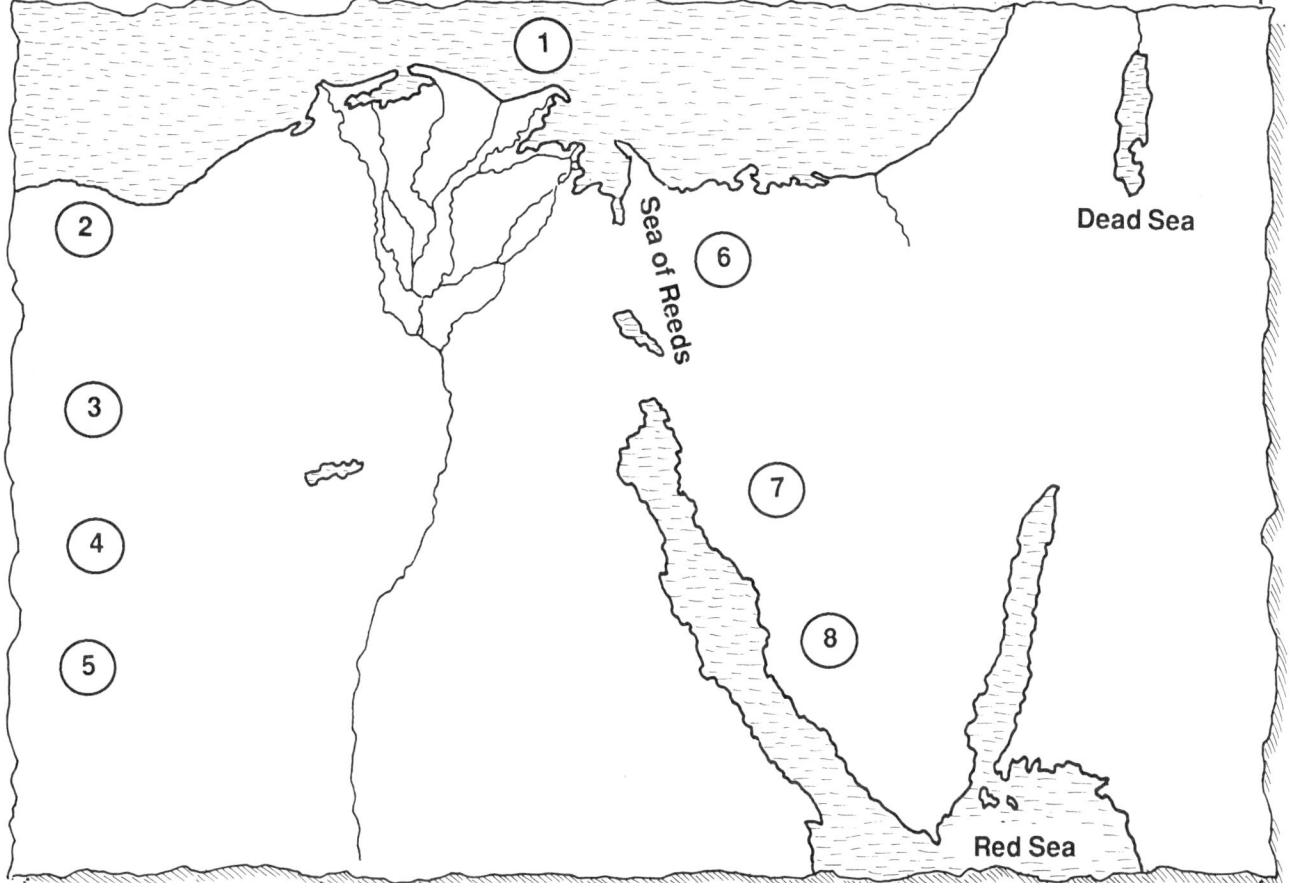

They lived happily in Egypt and grew in number.

God cared that His people were oppressed. Exodus: 3,9

But their troubles were not over! The Egyptians followed the Hebrews. Exodus 14

God told Moses to ask the Pharaoh to let the Hebrews leave Egypt. Pharaoh said, "NO!" Exodus 3:10; Exodus 5:3.

Over the land of Egypt, there were plagues: water turned to blood there were frogs and lice and ... Exodus 8-10

Joseph brought his brothers and his father, Jacob, to Egypt. Genesis 37-50

A new Pharaoh made the Hebrews slaves. Exodus 1

One night, after a special meal, the Hebrews escaped. Exodus 11; Exodus 12: 29-36

The Passover Seder

Focus **To identify the links between the Seder and the story of Moses.**

Passover is the time for a special family meal, the Seder. The food at the Seder tells the story of slavery or oppression and freedom, e.g. the bitter herbs are a reminder of the bitter times as slaves. It is a celebration of freedom but also a time to remember that even today, not everyone is free.

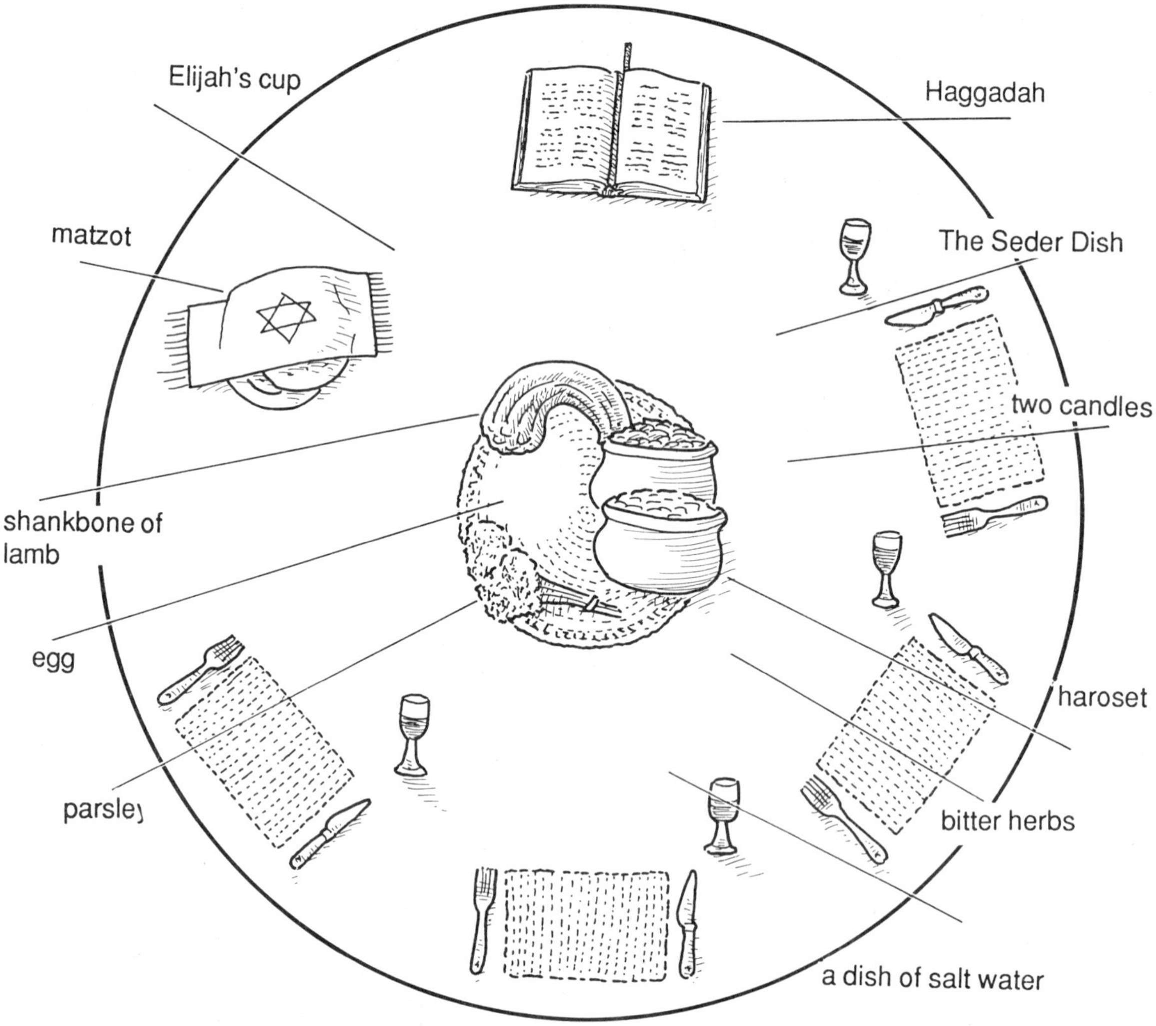
Elijah's cup
Haggadah
matzot
The Seder Dish
two candles
shankbone of lamb
egg
haroset
parsley
bitter herbs
a dish of salt water

Activities

- Draw in what is missing from the table at the Passover Seder.
- Read Exodus 12 and 13 and:
  - Colour in blue at least two foods eaten by the Hebrews before they escaped.
  - Colour in green at least two foods which are reminders of the bitterness of slavery.
- Why do Jews eat matzot or unleavened bread?
- If you were Jewish, what would your thoughts and feelings be at the Seder?

Extra Idea

In some countries minority groups are still oppressed. Collect newspaper reports about this subject for a discussion and display.

Rosh Hashanah and Yom Kippur

Rosh Hashanah and Yom Kippur and the ten days in between them are called the Days of Awe. These are days to look back upon your past year in repentance for the wrong things you have done, and a time to look forward, to decide how you can be better next year.

ROSH HASHANAH

New Year

YOM KIPPUR

The Day of Atonement

Rosh Hashanah, or New Year, occurs in September or October. It marks the Birthday of the World.

One tradition tells that God has a Book of Life and at the end of the year, good people are inscribed in it. A traditional Rosh Hashanah greeting is: May you be inscribed for a good year!

In the synagogue, the story of Abraham and Isaac is read. It tells how Abraham was prepared to sacrifice his son to God. (Genesis 22: 1-18)

At Rosh Hashanah, apples dipped in honey or honey cake are eaten. Honey is a symbol of the hope for sweetness in the New Year.

Most of the day is spent in the synagogue. It is a time to feel especially close to God. It is a day of fasting, prayer and repentance.

Yom Kippur is the holiest day of the year. Jews fast from sunset to sunset on Yom Kippur. Nothing is eaten or drunk.

The rabbi wears a long white robe and the Torah scrolls are dressed in white. White is a symbol of purity.

At Yom Kippur, relatives who have died are remembered and special 'yahrzeit' candles are lit in their memory.

Activities

- Why do you think the story of Abraham and Isaac is a good story for Rosh Hashanah?
- New years begin on different dates. Find out when these happen this year:

  - New school year _____
  - Secular New Year _____
  - Jewish New Year _____
  - Chinese New Year _____ .

- What symbols, food or other items might be appropriate symbols for a new year?
- Design your own 'Book of Life' for this year. What do you think has been good about your life? What could be improved?

Shavuot

At Shavuot, the Jewish community celebrates the giving of the Torah, especially the Ten Commandments. These are rules for life - to help a group of people live together as a community.

The Ten Commandments are an agreement, or covenant, between God and the Jewish people. They begin: *"I am the Lord thy God"* .

Moses brought the Ten Commandments to the people on tablets of stone, and these have become symbolic shapes, often seen on the walls of synagogues.

Activities

- Working in pairs, discuss the Commandments (see Exodus 20).
- Divide them into two groups:
  (1) Commandments about God
  (2) Commandments about how to live.
  Write them on the two tablets below.

** Discuss **

- Do people keep these Commandments today?
- Find examples of stories and pictures (your own or from newspapers) to support your view.

Commandments about God   **Commandments about how to live**

New guidelines

Focus To consider the effect of a Charter of Rights and Responsibilities upon a community.

At Shavuot, the Jewish community celebrates the giving of the Torah - the rules for life. Imagine that you are stranded on an island with twenty other people. You will be there for some time so you have to agree a Charter of Rights and Responsibilities as guidelines for your community.

Activities

- Choose five 'rules' that are important to you.
- Share your 'rules' with a group of four people.
- Agree on six rules. Write them out.

- As a class, try to agree on ten important rules. Display them on the wall. You could use the Declaration of Human Rights or the Children's Charter to help.
- What will happen if people do not keep the rules?

NOW

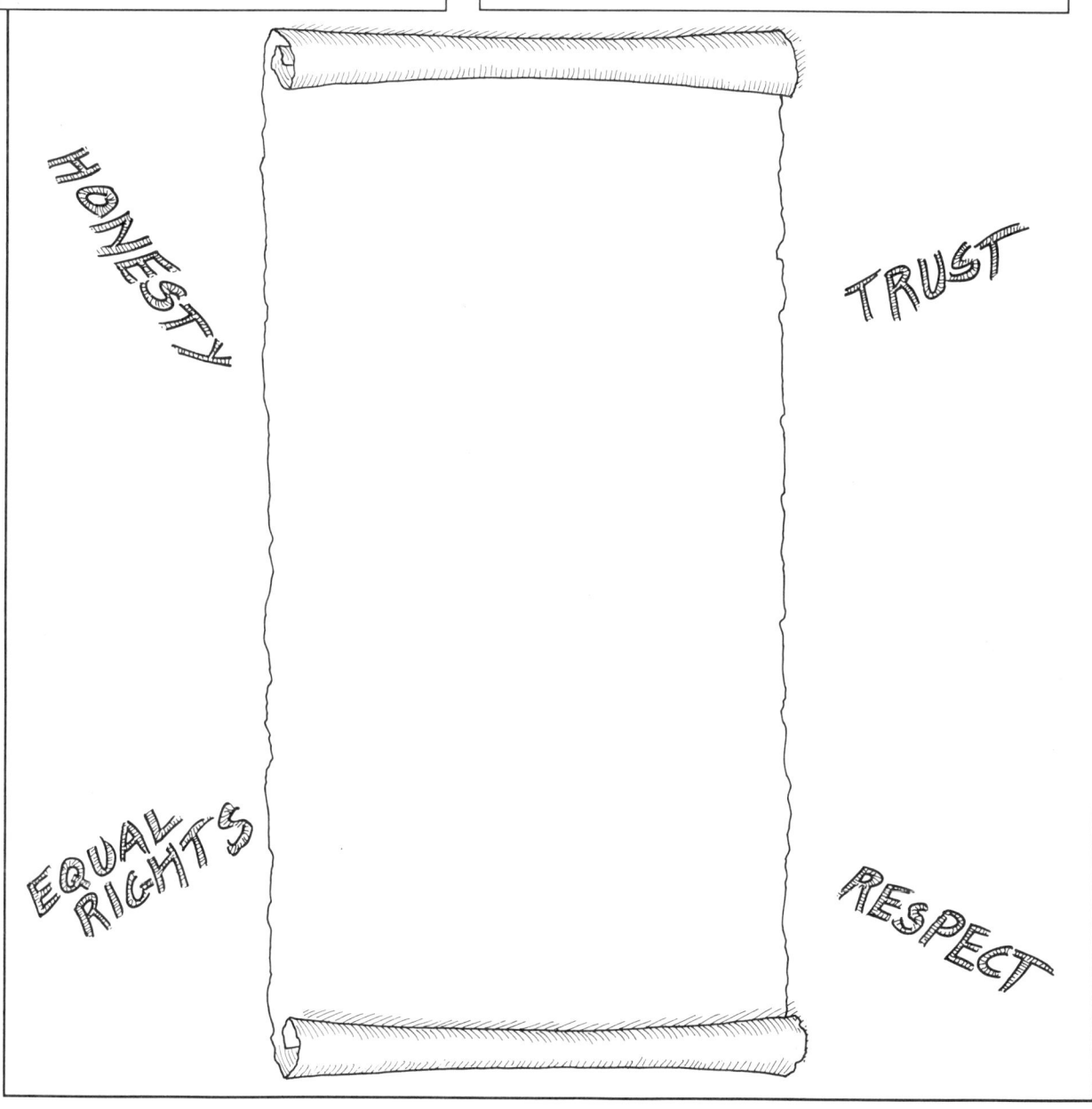

HONESTY

TRUST

EQUAL RIGHTS

RESPECT

Sukkot

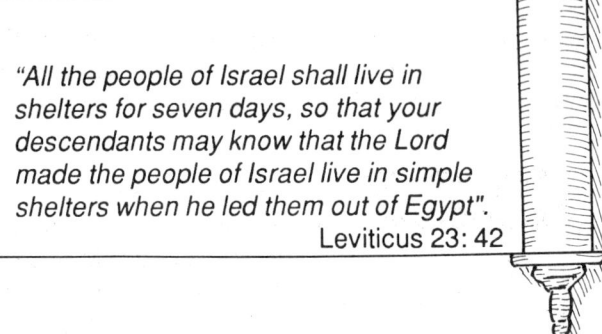

"All the people of Israel shall live in shelters for seven days, so that your descendants may know that the Lord made the people of Israel live in simple shelters when he led them out of Egypt".
Leviticus 23: 42

A sukkah is a building with three closed sides, the fourth being open to allow entry. The roof is made from twigs or bamboo poles, interwoven with greenery. You should be able to see the stars and feel the rain through the roof. It symbolises humans' dependence on God.

Activities

- Make a model sukkah from a shoe-box or a larger version using school screens.

  You will need:

  a shoe-box/3 screens
  bamboo sticks/long twigs
  greenery
  fruits to hang in the sukkah
  cards showing Jewish symbols.

- Write some display notes for your sukkah using the questions on the pad below.

Sukkah made from screens.

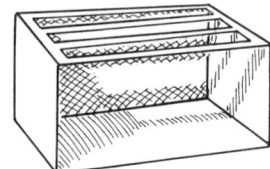

Explain the following:

Why do Jews build a sukkah?

Where is it usually built?

What do you do in a sukkah and why?

Why do you hang fruit inside?

What does the 'open' roof symbolise?

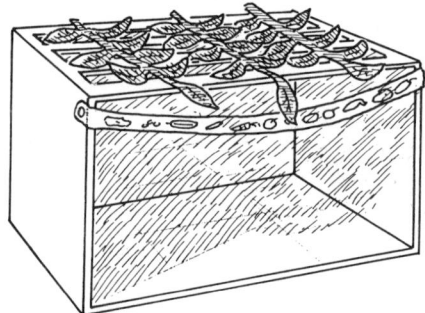

Sukkah made from a shoe box.

The lulav

To understand that the waving of the lulav fulfils the Commandments and symbolises God's presence.

At Sukkot, a lulav (a wand made from a palm branch, two willow branches and three myrtle branches) and an etrog, a fruit like a lemon, are waved in six directions - front, right, back, left, up and down. This symbolises God's power everywhere.

"On that day take some of the best fruit from your trees, take palm branches and the branches of leafy trees, and begin a religious festival to honour the Lord your God"

Leviticus 23: 40

Activities

● Make a lulav using natural greenery or card and crêpe paper **or** make a group collage of a lulav.

You will need:

a palm branch/green card
2 willow branches/green crêpe paper
3 myrtle branches or similar (privet)/green crêpe paper
cream card (woven) for the 'raffia' lulav holder
raffia for trying the branches
a lemon.

● Write some display notes for your lulav using the questions on the pad below.

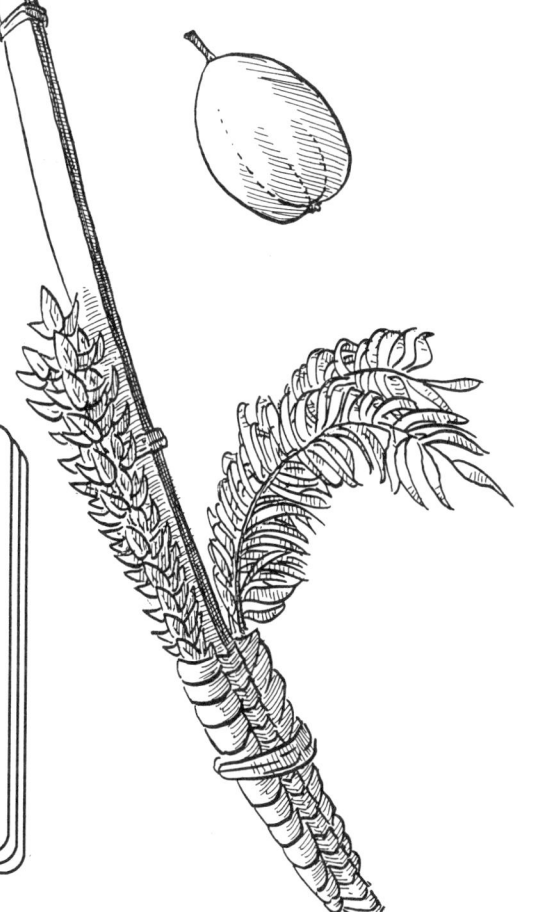

Explain the following:

What are the three plants or species which make up the lulav?
What do you do with the lulav and etrog?
What do these actions symbolise?

Extra Idea

The four species symbolise the four elements and the parts of a person used in the worship of God. Write labels and draw pictures to explain the symbolic meanings. Attach these to your lulav.

OBJECT	ELEMENT	BODY PARTS
etrog	fire	heart
palm	air	spine
myrtle	earth	eyes
willow	water	lips

Simchat Torah

To appreciate the unending cycle of reading the Torah and the joy of the festival.

The title at the top of this sheet means 'Rejoicing in the Torah'.

On Simchat Torah, the scrolls of the Torah are processed around the synagogue.

Activity

- Make 2 scrolls.
  You could use:
  2 sheets of white paper (A4), rolled
  4 pieces of dowelling for the rollers
  strong glue.

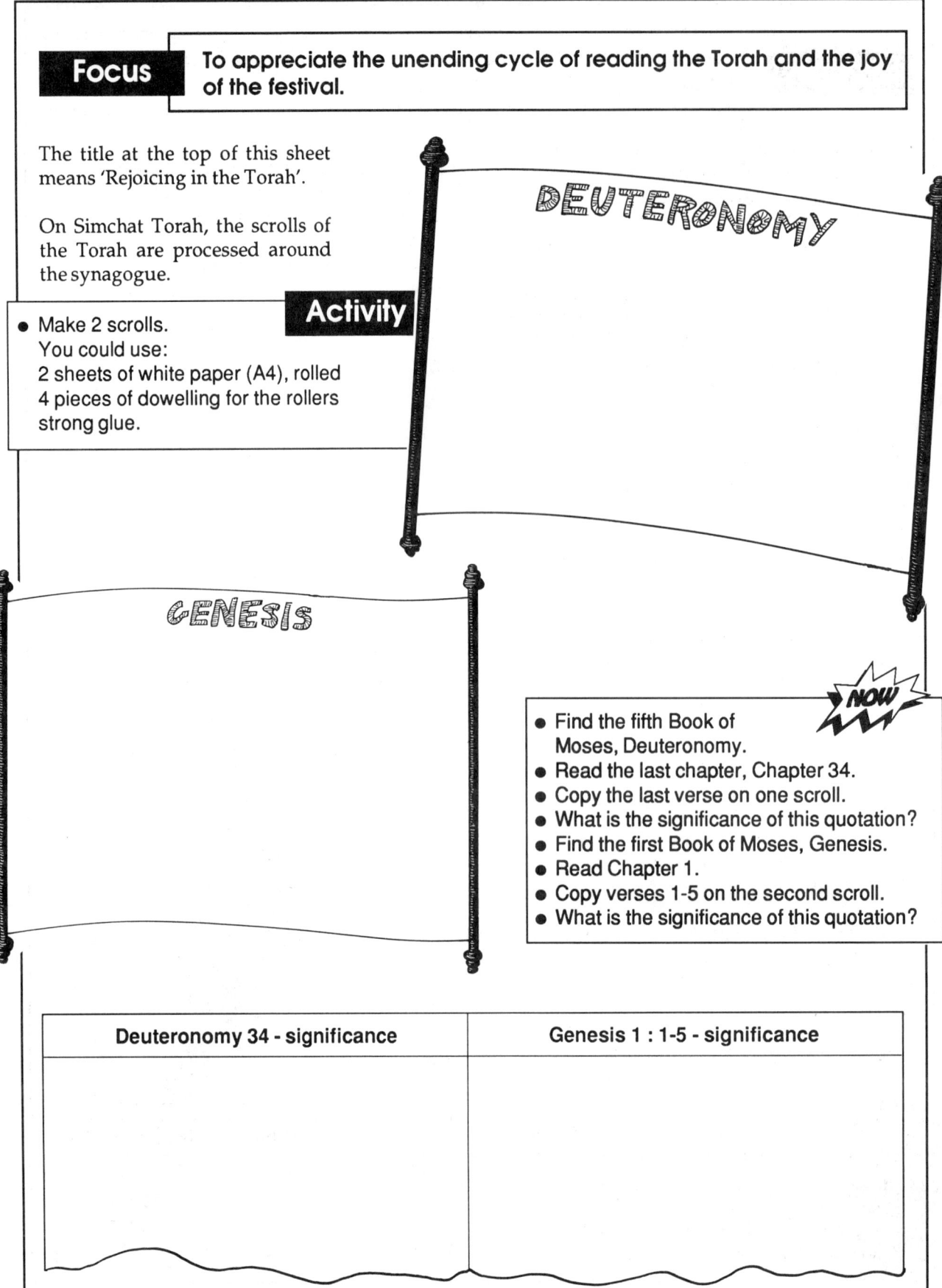

DEUTERONOMY

GENESIS

NOW

- Find the fifth Book of Moses, Deuteronomy.
- Read the last chapter, Chapter 34.
- Copy the last verse on one scroll.
- What is the significance of this quotation?
- Find the first Book of Moses, Genesis.
- Read Chapter 1.
- Copy verses 1-5 on the second scroll.
- What is the significance of this quotation?

Deuteronomy 34 - significance	Genesis 1 : 1-5 - significance

Hanukah (1)

Focus To discuss the themes of freedom to worship and the Jewish belief in God's power.

Hanukah is a festival of rededication.

continue over the page ...

Mattathias

The story of Judah the Maccabee

The Syrian King, Antiochus, captured the land of Israel. He forbade the Jews to worship God in their own way. He tried to make them worship idols, eat pig flesh and forbade them to study the Torah or to keep the Sabbath laws.

Mattathias, an old priest, stood before a Syrian soldier and said, "Neither I, nor my sons, nor any faithful Jew will ever worship any idols ..."

Mattathias led his five sons and other faithful men to the mountains to form a small army to fight the Syrians. When Mattathias died, his son Judah, with God's help, led this army to victory over the powerful Syrians.

Activity

- Imagine that you are Mattathias speaking to the crowd. Explain your feelings about Antiochus' rules. Try to encourage people to join your army.

Hanukah (2)

Focus — To discuss the hanukiah as a symbol of rededication and of religious freedom and to see how Hanukah can be enjoyed.

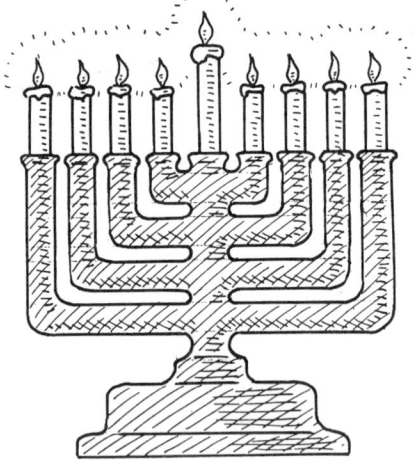

"Blessed are You, O Lord our God, King of the Universe who have given us life, sustained us, and enabled us to reach this joyous season."

Festival blessing

For the eight days of Hanukah, the hanukiah or Hanukah Menorah, is placed in a window as a symbol of religious freedom. A hanukiah is a row of eight candles with a ninth, the shamash, which is used to light the others, set apart from the rest.

Activities

- Remind yourselves of the story of Judah the Maccabee.
- Discuss what the lights of the candles symbolise at this festival.
- You could make a hanukiah from a piece of wood with clay or foil 'cups' to hold the candles (see the picture below). Or you could make it using a 'stained glass' effect and display the hanukiah in the window of the classroom (see the picture above). You will need card for a template, 2 sheets of black card and tissue paper: white for candles, yellow for flames, blue for the hanukiah itself.

Extra Idea

The Hebrew letters on the dreidel stand for 'Nes gadol haya sham' - 'A great miracle happened here'.
Why do people play this game at Hanukah?

To make a simple dreidel:
Cut a square out of card.
Mark on the Hebrew letters.
Place a matchstick or cocktail stick through the centre.

To play:
Each player starts with the same number of counters.
To start, each player puts one counter into the kitty.
Each player spins the dreidel.

Each player has to do what the dreidel says:
Put a counter in.
Take half.
Winner takes all!
Nothing!

The winner is the person who ends up with all the counters!

Put a counter in.

Take half.

Winner takes all!

Nothing!

Purim

To appreciate the serious message behind the festival.

Activity

● Read the story of Purim in the Book of Esther. Fill in the missing names in the story below.

Characters:

King Ahasuerus

Mordecai, a Jew who helped Ahasuerus

Queen Esther, Mordecai's niece

Haman, Prime Minister to Ahasuerus

The Story of Esther

King _____ ruled Persia and lived in the capital Shushan. He was married to Queen _____ .

_____ was Prime Minister and a wicked man. He wanted everyone to bow down to him. Mordecai refused because _____ wore an image of an idol on his coat. _____ was so angry, he planned to kill Mordecai and other Jews eleven months from that day.

When Mordecai heard about the plan, he begged Queen _____ to help. He said, "If you keep silent, all your relatives will die." By law no one was allowed to approach the King without permission and _____ was afraid. All the Jews in Shushan fasted for three days and prayed for _____ .
She then invited the King and _____ to a banquet. King _____ was so pleased he offered _____ anything she wanted. She invited them to a second banquet.

This time she begged the King, "Let my life and the life of my people be saved for there is a plot to kill us." The King thus discovered _____'s plan and ordered his execution. The Jewish people in Shushan were safe!

Mordecai ordered all generations to keep the Feast of Purim!

● Talk about the message behind this festival. Why do people celebrate it every year?
● Create a drama script from the story and perform it in an assembly.

NOW

Purim celebration

To appreciate the joy of the ritual and the serious message behind the festival of Purim.

In the synagogue at Purim, the Book of Esther is read from a scroll, the Megillah. Each time the name of Esther is heard, everyone cheers. At the name of Haman everyone 'boos', stamps their feet and shakes a gregger.

Activity

To make a gregger you need:

square pieces of card
dried peas or beans
tape.

- Fold the card into a triangle.
- Fill with beans.
- Tape the edges.
- Decorate with Jewish symbols.

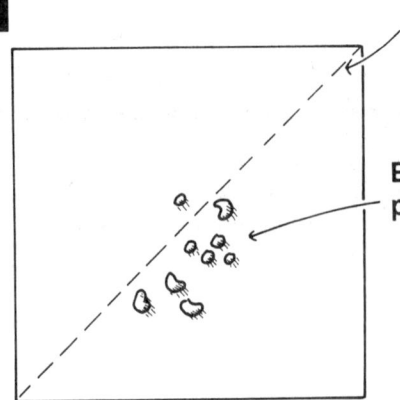

Bend and crease

Fold

Beans and peas

Tape along the edges

" Discuss "

- Are there Hamans and Esthers in the world today?
- Why are rituals such as the shaking of a gregger and the eating of special foods important for certain festivals?

It is traditional to eat *Hamantaschen*, 'Haman's purses' or 'Haman's ears'! They are triangular-shaped pastries.

Hamantaschen

Pastry
5oz margarine
5oz sugar
4oz self raising flour
1 egg

Filling
4 oz poppy seeds, ground
grated lemon rind
1/4 pint water
2oz sugar
1oz margarine
1oz sultanas
Simmer ingredients in
water until thick. Cool.

Method
Cream the margarine and sugar
Add the egg and flour
Mix to a stiff dough
Knead
Cut into 10cm circles
Add the filling
Pinch the edges to make triangles
Brush with honey.

Cook for 12 to 15
minutes at Gas
mark 4-5
Electric 375 degrees
or 180 degrees C.

Tu Bi-Shevat

To appreciate the tree as a symbol of life and hope for the future.

Tu Bi-Shevat is the festival of New Year for trees.

A wise rabbi was walking along a road when he saw a man planting a tree. The rabbi asked how long it would take for the tree to bear fruit. He was told seventy years. The rabbi asked if the man hoped to live that long. The man replied, 'I found a fruitful world because my forefathers planted for me. So I will do the same for my children.'

(*Midrash*)

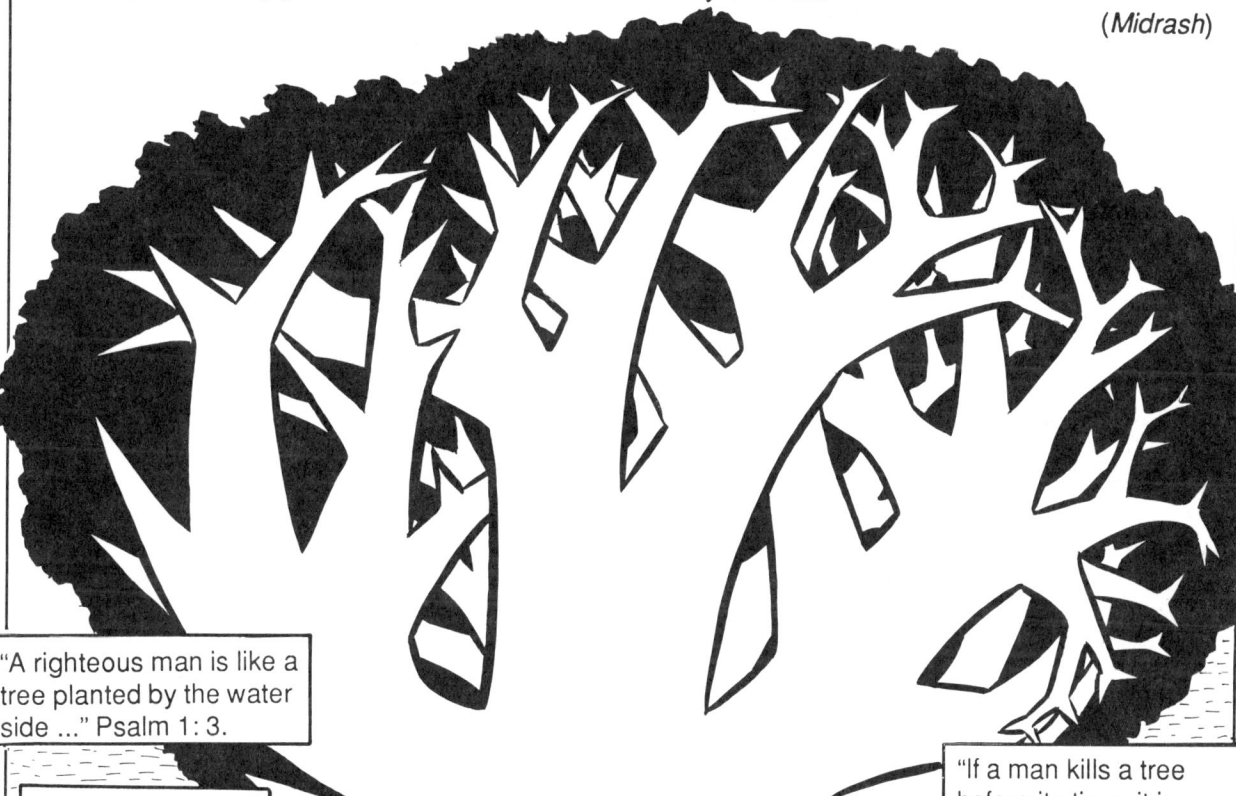

"A righteous man is like a tree planted by the water side ..." Psalm 1: 3.

The Torah is called 'The Tree of Life'.

Trees are planted in Israel to reclaim the land ...

... or as memorials to people who have died.

... or for those who risked their lives to save Jews in the war.

"If a man kills a tree before its time, it is as though he had murdered a soul. " Rabbi Nachman of Bratzlav.

Branches cut from trees hold a wedding canopy.

Eating fruits from the trees celebrates God's creation.

Planting a tree in Israel links you to the land.

Activity

- People plant trees for different reasons. They have different feelings and hopes. Imagine you are planting a tree on Tu Bi-Shevat. Add your feelings and your hopes to the branches above.

Teachers' notes

SIKH FESTIVALS

There are two types of Sikh festivals: 'melas', which have the characteristics of fairs, and 'gurpurbs' which are the anniversaries of the birth or death of the Gurus.

Baisakhi and Diwali are two examples of 'melas'. Baisakhi marks the beginning of the Sikh New Year and occurs on 13th April. The main celebrations take place on the Sunday following this date. At Baisakhi, the story of Guru Gobind Singh is told and the birth of the Khalsa or Sikh Brotherhood remembered. It is also a time when new members are initiated into the Khalsa. The ceremony of wearing the five Ks and taking Amrit, led by five Sikhs representing the Panj Pyare or Beloved Five, is reminiscent of the original event. Baisakhi is also the time of the wheat harvest in the Punjab.

Diwali is frequently taught in schools as a Hindu festival. It is important to note that it is also celebrated by Sikhs, although a very different story is told at the festival. The Sikh festival celebrates a story of deliverance or freedom. Since Guru Hargobind was concerned to secure the freedom of the fifty-two Hindu princes imprisoned with him, there are also strong elements of equal rights for all, irrespective of religious background. This teaching of equality is a feature of Sikhism. The festival is celebrated with bonfires and fireworks.

Guru Nanak's Birthday is an example of a 'gurpurb'. Guru Nanak is remembered as the 'founder' of Sikhism although he did not intend in his teaching to found a new religion, rather to turn others to a more spiritual way of life.

Prior to the festival, there will be an Akhand Path, a continuous reading of the Guru Granth Sahib, the holy book. This will take two days, read by different women and men in two-hour relays. As the reading draws to a close early in the morning, the festival day begins.

Sikh festivals are celebrated in the gurdwara with hymns, prayers and stories about the Gurus, with a langar or meal for all who attend and, as in the case of Baisakhi, festivities and dancing in the open air.

Page 45. BAISAKHI

Questions refer to a need for courage in those who become members of the Khalsa, a name meaning 'pure' or 'dedicated' ones. Originally, the men had to decide whether they were to become dedicated Sikhs and continue the fight for independence against the Moghul rulers.

Issues of faith in God and trust in the Guru are important here. Questions raise a wider issue of why some people align themselves with a religious tradition when others do not. Answers could include reference to the meanings of the names, e.g. Singh - lion - a feeling of strength, power. Or they could relate to a feeling of belonging to a community. The person prepares by allowing the hair to grow, then by wearing the five Ks and taking Amrit. Issues include - what obligations would be upon someone and how they would cope with being conspicuous in their religious dress.

Page 46. SIKH SYMBOLS

There are slightly different meanings attributed to the symbols in different sources.

KESH - symbol of dedication to God.

KIRPAN - symbol of a willingness to defend truth and justice.

KHANDA - the two edges symbolise right behaviour in spiritual and daily life.

KANGA - symbol of cleanliness and discipline.

KACHS - symbol of modesty and readiness for action.

KARA PARSHAD - eating this symbolises equality.

KARA - the circle of steel is a symbol of God's eternity and of strength and unity.

AMRIT - sprinkled on the hair and eyes and drunk, this symbolises belonging to the Khalsa.

Page 47. DIWALI

This tests understanding of Sikh teaching on equality and the need for actions to support belief.

Page 48. GURU NANAK'S BIRTHDAY

Stress that the Guru's teaching is the foundation for Sikh belief and practice. Guru Nanak is often shown meditating upon God, for repeating the divine name is part of Sikh practice. Pupils should notice this attitude of meditation from the picture.

Baisakhi

The story of Baisakhi

Baisakhi marks the birth of the Khalsa, or Sikh Brotherhood. In AD 1699, Guru Gobind Singh, the tenth Guru, spoke to a large gathering of Sikhs at Anandpur.

He asked them, "Is there anyone here who would give his head for his Guru?" After some time, one man stepped forward. The Guru took him into his tent. Then the Guru reappeared alone, blood dripping from his sword. He asked the same question again. Eventually a second man stepped forward, and he too was taken into the tent. This happened three more times. Then the Guru revealed the five men alive. They were all wearing turbans and the five Ks just like the Guru.

The Guru called them the Panj Pyare, the Beloved Five. They, the Guru and his wife shared Amrit (sugar crystals dissolved in water) as a symbol of belonging to the Khalsa.

Baisakhi is celebrated on 13th April in Britain. It is a time when women and men join the Khalsa. Five Sikhs take the role of the Panj Pyare and lead the initiation ceremony.

Activities

- Talk about the following issues:
  - What sort of people do you think Guru Gobind Singh was looking for to form a community?
  - What do you think made the five men step forward when others were afraid?
- Sikh men take the name 'Singh' meaning 'lion'. Sikh women take the name 'Kaur' meaning princess.
  - What do you think this shows?
  - How might you feel if you shared one of these names?
- Label the five Ks in the diagram. What do they signify?

Extra Ideas

Look back at the story.
What do you think happens when someone joins the Khalsa?
Do some research.
Would membership of the Khalsa be easy?
How might it affect your daily life?

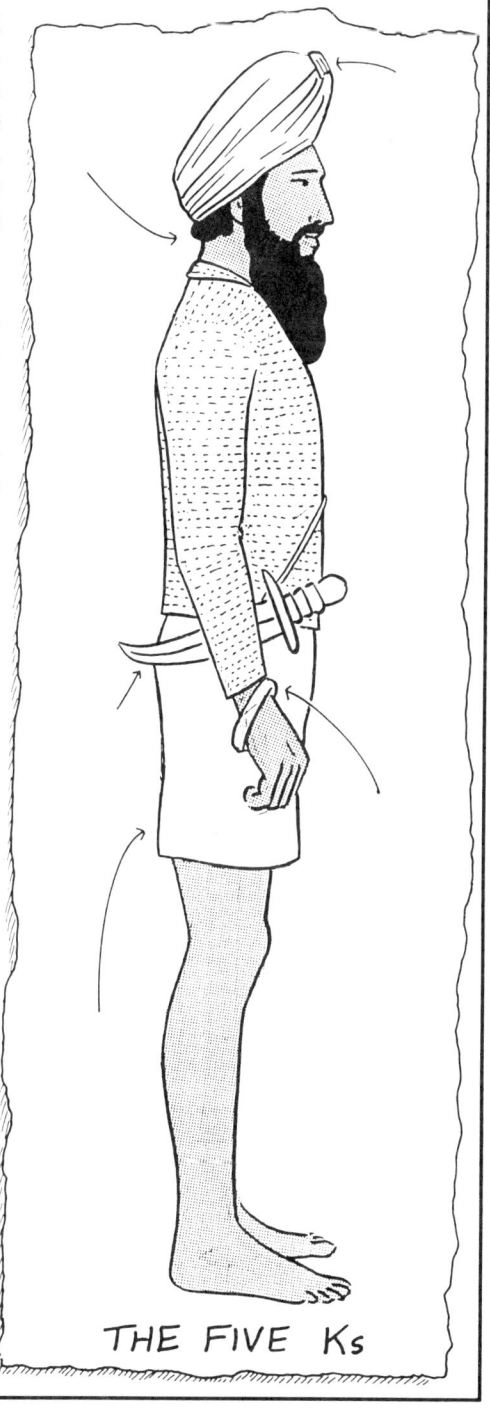

THE FIVE Ks

Sikh symbols

- The symbols in the left-hand column and the meanings are jumbled. Match these important Sikh symbols with their meanings
- Write one fact about each symbol in the box to show how it is used.

Activities

1 **KESH**	**A** Symbol of a willingness to defend truth and justice.	
2 **KIRPAN**	**B** Symbol of cleanliness and discipline.	
3 **KHANDA**	**C** Symbol of God's eternity and of strength and unity.	
4 **KANGA**	**D** Eating this symbolises equality.	
5 **KACHS**	**E** The two edges symbolise right behaviour in spiritual and daily life.	
6 **KARA PARSHAD**	**F** Symbol of modesty and readiness for action.	
7 **KARA**	**G** Symbol of dedication to God.	
8 **AMRIT**	**H** Sprinkled on the hair and eyes and drunk, this symbolises belonging to the Khalsa.	

After worshipping together, Sikhs eat Kara Parshad, a sweet mixture made from semolina, sugar, butter and water. Eating together shows that everyone is equal before God.

Kara Parshad

You will need:

1 cup of semolina
1 cup of clarified butter
1 cup of sugar
2 cups of water

Method
Boil the water and sugar until dissolved.
Heat the semolina and butter.
Add the sugar mixture.
Serve warm.

Diwali

To learn about Sikh teaching on the equality of all before God and the importance of actions.

Diwali is a Sikh festival about equality and deliverance.

> "... regard all men as equal."
> Guru Nanak

> "It is through actions that some come near God."
> Guru Nanak

Guru Hargobind, the sixth Guru, was imprisoned by the Emperor Jehangir. He was held in the Gwalior Fort with fifty-two Hindu princes.

The Emperor agreed to release Guru Hargobind but the Guru would only leave with the princes.

Emperor Jehangir said only those who could hold on to the Guru's cloak could leave with him.

The Guru had a long cloak with fifty-two silk tassels brought to him. Holding on to the tassels, the princes walked with the Guru though the narrow corridors to freedom.

Activity

● Cover your cloak with a modern story on the same theme, either one of your own or one from a newspaper.

" Discuss "

■ Freedom for all? If you were a Sikh, how might the story of Guru Hargobind change the way you live?

continue over the page...

Guru Nanak's birthday

Focus — To understand why Guru Nanak has been and continues to be an important person for Sikhs.

On his birthday, Sikhs read their holy book, the Guru Granth Sahib, hold processions and tell stories about the life and teaching of Guru Nanak. He is remembered for his teachings about God (he believed God had called him to teach others) and about how people should live their lives.

Here are some of Guru Nanak's teachings and sayings:

I was a minstrel out of work
The Lord gave me employment
The mighty One instructed me,
'Night and day, sing my praise.'

... regard all men as equal.

There is no rich, no poor,
no black and no white, before
God. It is your actions that
make you good or bad.

It is through actions
that some come near to God
and some wander away.

To love God you
must first learn to
love each other.

... actions will speak in
God's court. Without
good deeds, none will
find the way.

The Lord of all the
people is One.

Remember God, work
hard and help others.

Guru Nanak
The Mool Mantra

There is one God,
Eternal Truth is His name
Maker of all things,
Fearing nothing and at enmity with nothing ...

Activity

- Imagine you are a Sikh and that it is Guru Nanak's Birthday. Write a short talk to explain to children why Guru Nanak is so important to you. You can use his teachings, tell a story about his life or explain how his picture shows the sort of person he was.